The Smith House
History Cookbook

By Freida Welch-Bafile

The Smith House History Cook Book

By Freida Welch-Bafile

Copyright © 2015 by Freida Welch-Bafile

Published by
The Smith House
84 South Chestatee Street
Dahlonega, GA 30533
706-867-7000
www.SmithHouse.com

ISBN 978-0-692-54748-9

Although we have made an effort to publish only accurate material in the public domain or material we have been given permission to reproduce, neither the Smith House nor the author can assume responsibility for facts, judgments, opinions, or errors made by resources used for research.

Recipes

Recipe for Love 3
The Remedy: The Shine 118

Soups and Salads
Smith House Summer Salad 27
Smith House Cabbage Salad 27
Smith House Coleslaw 27
Three Sisters Salad 29
Cranberry Salad 29
Strawberry or Blueberry Salad 29
The Smith House Abee Apple Salad........ 31
Lettuce and Boiled Egg Salad 31
Apple-Pineapple Slaw 31
ABC Soup................................ 33
Conee-Banee Soup 35
Hearty Beef Stew........................ 35

Meats
Smith House Southern Fried Chicken...... 43
Smith House Fried Chicken Tenders....... 43
Buttermilk Baked Chicken 43
Smith House Baked Chicken 45
Party Chicken Salad 45
Smith House Roast Beef.................. 45
Evan's Wings-n-Things................... 46
Smith House Thanksgiving Turkey 47
Smith House Baked Ham 47
Country Fried Steak 49
Sweet and Sour Meatballs 49
Barbecue Pork 49
Fried Shrimp 51
Boiled Shrimp 51
Tarter Sauce 51
Cocktail Sauce 51

Vegetables
Smith House Creamed Corn................ 57
Skillet Corn 57
Smith House Cabbage Casserole 59
Smith House Squash Casserole............ 59
Smith House Black-eyed Peas 61
Baked Beans............................. 61
Green Bean Casserole.................... 63
Smith House Green Beans................. 63
Creamy Mashed Potatoes 65
Thanksgiving Rice dish 65
Candied Sweet Potatoes 67
Smith House Macaroni and Cheese......... 67
Smith House Candied Yams 69
Sweet Potato Casserole 69
Smith House Fried Okra 71
Broccoli and Rice Casserole 71
Smith House Turnip or Collard Greens ... 73
Smith House Lima Beans.................. 73

Breads
Smith House Yeast Rolls 77
Smith House Corn Muffins 77
Angel Biscuits 79
Sweet Potato Biscuits 79
Smith House Cinnamon Rolls 81
Smith House Sausage Rolls 81
Bill Fry's Lacy Cornbread 83
Crackling Corn Bread 83
Smith House Corn Bread Dressing 85
Easy Stuffing 85

Drinks
Iced Tea................................ 92
Tea Punch............................... 92
Smith House Sweet Tea 93
Smith House Un-Sweet Tea................ 93
Smith House Lemonade.................... 95
Smith House Peach Punch 95
Summer Tea Punch........................ 97
Strawberry Punch........................ 97

Relishes and Jellies
Smith House Squash Pickles............. 101
Smith House Cranberry Relish........... 101
Harvest Beets.......................... 101
Bread and Butter Pickles 103
Okra Pickles........................... 103
Muscadine Jelly........................ 103
Strawberry Jam 105
Moonshine Jelly........................ 105
Blueberry Jelly 105
Old Timey Chow-Chow Relish............. 107
Hot Pepper Jam......................... 107

Desserts
Old Fashioned Buttermilk Pie 85
Smith House Pumpkin Pie 111
Sweet Potato Cake...................... 111
Strawberry Pie 112
Smith House Strawberry Shortcake....... 113
Quick & Easy Strawberry Shortcake 113
Nanny's Strawberry Shortcake 115
Free Jim Apple Pie..................... 117
Smith House Pecan Pie 119
Thelma's Southern Pecan Pie 119
Smith House Banana Pudding 121
Ole Fashioned Banana Pudding 121
Smith House Fried Bananas 123
Baked Bananas 123
Blueberry Cobbler...................... 124
Smith House Peach Cobbler 124
Smith House Apple Cobbler 125
Smith House Strawberry Cobbler 125

Table of Contents

Preface 1
About the Author 2
History of Lumpkin County 4
History of The Smith House 6
Smith House Museum 16
Family Style Dining 22

Salads and Soups
Tomato: A fruit or vegetable? 26
The Three Sisters 28
The Famous who dined at The Smith House: Remembered by Doris Abee 30
Sequoya's Alphabet 32
ABC Soup 33
New Found Friends 34
A Love Story Goes Wrong 36

Meats
Beginning of the Smith House 42
Bear on the Square 44
The Turkey Run 46
Court's in Session 48
Destruction 50

Vegetables
Battlebranch Goldmine 56
A Three-Day Ration 58
A Twist of Fate 60
The Safety Man 62
They Called Her Amazon 64
Fred Welch Sr., Operator and Owner of the Smith House from 1946-1980 66
Fred Welch, Jr., Operator of the Smith House from 1970 - Present 68
There's Millions in It 70
Dahlonega Mint 72

Breads
Thelma Welch – Operator and Owner of The Smith House from 1946-1980 76
Thelma's Hospitality 78
William Benjamin Fry, Owner of the Smith House from 1946-1970 – It's 5 o'clock Somewhere 80
Effie Kate Fry 82
Buttermilk 84

Drinks
Southern Table Wine 92
The Present-day Smith House 94
Wedding on the Waves 96

Relishes and Jellies
The Second Welch Generation 100
The Welch Family's Third and Fourth Generations 102
The Art of Canning 104

Desserts
Who Murdered Mary? 110
William and Mary Lou Smith, Owners of the Smith House 1944-1946 112
Bakery Now Open 114
"Free Jim" 116
The Shiners 118
Wagon Trains 120
The Parade is Coming 122
Shirley Welch, Owner of the Smith House from 1970-Present 124
Gold Rush Days in Dahlonega – A Mountain Festival 126
Gold Rush Kings and Queens 127

Stamp Mills
Stamp Mills and the Frank Hall Stamp Mill 132
Picture Gallery of Old Dahlonega and its Gold Mining History 143
Thank You 153

Dedication

I dedicate this book to my family and this poem to emphasize the importance of togetherness and the seasons of change we experience in our lives.

> *Just as the earth goes through seasons, so does a family in the course of time endure seasons. Marriage, falling in love and the birth of a child are times of renewal like spring. Long pleasant periods of calm that some families are blessed to have are like the feelings of an endless summer. As we and our children grow older our leaves start to change. We start to experience autumn. This may seem like dying but it is really only signs of a new phase of life. The times of crises and hardship are times for the family to stay close together, help each other out and endure what are sometimes the frigid winds of change. This period is akin to winter. Life is full of seasons and changes which are best experienced with the support of friends and family.*
>
> Quote from http://www.familyfriendpoems.com/poems/family/

Preface

Walking Down Memory Lane

One pleasant summer day, I decided to take a stroll around the public square of Dahlonega. I was looking at the buildings and thinking about the history of each one. I thought about how each building played some part in the molding of this town. I started walking to the south part of town where Mount Hope cemetery is located. I have lived in Dahlonega all my life but never realized the historical significance of the people and the legacy they left behind. The cemetery is separated from the University of North Georgia by a gate, with the college on the other side.

I started down a couple of roads that wound around the different areas of the cemetery. I continued my walk, noticing the bright day and the cool breeze. I heard in the background the birds singing, as well as the college students talking as they were scurrying to class.

A gentle incline opened up to markers from different time frames on both sides of the path. I saw soldiers' graves; soldiers that fought in many different wars that shaped this country into what it is today. I was curious about the markers, standing like proud soldiers themselves peering out of the earth with no name or date markings. I wondered if any of these markers were miners who flocked here in the first Gold Rush in 1829.

Some of the families that are still living in Dahlonega are represented by their ancestors whose dates go back to the establishment of this town. I also saw small graves that were inscribed with names and dates as early as the 1800s that looked like someone had used a primitive tool to write with. Many tombstones were only large rocks used to mark the memorial of that person, with no name visible. Perhaps, over time, their names were washed away and the memory of their presence here forgotten. Some historical graves were well taken care of by their relatives, while others were neglected, with the markers crumbling into the earth. I tried to visualize what their lives were like in this town; how they dressed, acted, and what part they played in sculpting this old village.

I ended my walk by visiting my grandparents' lot. Studying all the dates on the markers, I realized that my family heritage dates back to the mid-1800s, as well. Behind me I saw the markers for the Fry family, who were instrumental in helping my grandparents during the beginning stages of the Smith House. I noticed they also had old roots in Dahlonega. The peace I felt as I walked through signified that my visit here was meant to be. This book honors the voices of those who have lived before us and the legacy they have left behind in this old village. I hope their stories are remembered and that those families with deep roots in Dahlonega will be proud of the legacy they have left behind.

About the Author

Freida Welch-Bafile

I was born into the Welch family in the summer of 1970, and have spent all of my life here at the Smith House. I remember my grandfather, Fred Welch, who would make weekly trips to the Atlanta farmer's market when vegetables were not available from the local farmers. The fresh vegetables that he bought had to be "worked up" for the weekend. I vividly remember myself as a child riding the school bus in the afternoons and approaching the Smith House for my departure, anxiously waiting to see the outcome of my afternoon. My grandfather would make his trips, and if his truck was sitting outside the restaurant, my afternoon was full of work stringing and snapping green beans. He would inspect the strings, and if there was too much bean still left he would say, "There is one more bite off that bean." If his truck was not there, my afternoon was free to visit my friends on the town square. My favorite thing to do in the afternoons at the Smith House was to head to the kitchen and grab a snack, usually a chicken leg and a roll, and then visit my friends on the square of Dahlonega. I would visit a particular couple who owned a candle shop because they let me make candles out of the leftover wax.

My grandmother mostly worked with the local farmers and frequently traveled to their farms to pick up produce. One of my great aunt's fondest memories was when my grandmother took her to an apple farm for a picking. My grandmother pulled my grandfather's truck up to the trees and both would climb into the back of the truck and pick the apples from the trees.

Thelma and Jackie before apple picking

My mother, Shirley Welch, opened a bakery called the Sugar Shack in the old Hope House at the upper lot of the Smith House. My brother and I would come early in the mornings with our mother so she could bake her fresh breakfast items for the locals. Behind the house, Buck and Gladys Woods ran a panning box. They would let me pan for gold and also show guests how to extract the gold from the pan.

I met many interesting people that worked at the Smith House during my life, and the most interesting to me were two bakers that made all of the restaurant's baked goods, Ed Anderson and Estelle Patterson. Ed usually made the yeast rolls, and while he was mixing the dough in the large mixers, I would hide and stick my finger in the gooey ingredients and eat it. He would laugh and scold me at the same time. Estelle, while she was waiting on her baked goods in the oven, always sat on a stool and watched me and Ed fighting over the raw mix. She would point to Ed my whereabouts when I would hide from him.

Another memorable pair was Vedel Tanner and Vernell Davis, who was our fry cooks for many years. Vernell fried the chicken and Vedel fried the bananas. We are well known for our fried chicken, but the fried bananas were amazing. I was also an entrepreneur in my younger years, and noticing how people loved to buy honey, I decided to set up a stand outside to sell honey to the public. However, the local bee population did not appreciate my business skills and, therefore, decided to attack me by stinging my fingers multiple times. Vedel heard of my incident and immediately treated me with her herbal remedy. She took out of her mouth a heaping load of "snuff" and wrapped my finger in it. "Snuff" is finely ground chewing tobacco that is placed in the front part of the lip, not to be swallowed. Miraculously, it drew the stinger out of my finger and somehow made me feel better. I probably skipped supper that night thinking about the ointment on my hand. Back then, a lot of the older women I knew used "snuff," and a visible ring around their mouths proved it.

Now that I am all grown up, I am still making memories with the people I meet here at the Smith House. I love to hear the stories from visitors of my family's hospitality. A house is a home when there is love. The Smith House has been a good home to me because of all the memories and the love showed to me from the people who have either worked or stayed awhile with us. I am proud of my family's heritage and the legacy they have left behind. I thank my family for giving me so many precious memories, and hopefully they will be expressed in this book.

My family is the seed of my life that will never stop growing.

Recipe for Love

1 handful of sunscreen of love
1 grassy field
½ dozen children
2 or 3 small dogs
A pinch of a brook or stream
Some small pebbles

Mix the dogs and children together well and put them in the grassy field, stirring constantly. Apply sunscreen of love to combat the blistering heat of the sun. Pour the brook over the pebbles. Sprinkle the field with flowers. Spread all under a deep blue sky and bake in the hot sun. When brown, remove the children and place in a cool bathtub with lots of suds. Let the children rest in their beds with a nice bedtime story.

History of Lumpkin County

In 1828, gold was discovered in Dahlonega by Benjamin Parks while he was deer hunting at the Calhoun Mine. He accidentally kicked a rock and examined it to be gold. News of his find quickly spread, and the excitement rose so much that many people from far-off regions came here to "strike it rich." Travelers came on foot, horseback, and wagons and most were stricken by the thoughts of gold and acted madly. There were men panning in the streams and digging holes in the hillsides. The miner's philosophy was "if I found it then it was mine."

Briar Patch Mine, 1900
Vanishing Georgia, Georgia Archives, University System of Georgia

Many disputes between the Cherokee Indians and miners occurred as miners would sneak onto Indian land and mine their gold. A law was passed to prohibit mining on the land but was overlooked by both miners and Indians. The government sent troops to run off the miners, but they soon saw the potential revenue the gold would bring to the state. The Cherokee lands were distributed to the people of the state by means of a land lottery system, and ten counties were made out of this one area. It was the responsibility of the state to parcel out the lands as soon as possible. The name of the area became Lumpkin County in honor of the governor who removed the Indians.

In April 1833, an election was held for the purpose of determining what town would be the county seat, either Auraria or Dahlonega. Dahlonega was chosen to be the county seat because the "lot" on which the principal part of Auraria was located had been fraudulently drawn in the land lottery, therefore the title was defective. The area in Dahlonega was a central location from all areas of the gold region. The first Superior Court session voted the name of the settlement as "Talonega," from the Cherokee word meaning "yellow rock," and eventually this name turned into Dahlonega. There was so much gold mined in the area that in 1838 a branch of the United States mint was established in Dahlonega. The mint's records showed that over $6,000,000 was coined here until

Dahlonega Courthouse on the Public Square

Harper's New Monthly Magazine, Vol. 59, Issue 352 (September 1879).

Mule team bringing mining equipment to
Consolidated Gold Mine from Gainesville, GA.
Vanishing Georgia, Georgia Archives, University System of Georgia

the break out of the Civil War in 1861. The marking of the Dahlonega coin is known by the letter D above the date. The other branches were in New Orleans, Louisiana and Charlotte, North Carolina. The parent mint was located in Philadelphia. However, the discovery of gold in California in 1848 caused a decline in the gold production in the area, with plans to abolish the Dahlonega mint. During the Civil War, the machinery became damaged from exposure and unfit for further use as a mint. Federal soldiers occupied the mint and turned it into barracks for quartering the soldiers. The government withdrew from re-establishing a mint and donated the buildings and lands to the Trustees of North Georgia College for the purpose of education. Price Memorial on the campus sits on top of the original mint's foundation. The steeple, which showcases Dahlonega gold, tops the building as a reminder of the gold mined during those old Gold Rush days.

When the gold rush in Georgia was believed to be over, many miners headed west to join the 1849 California Gold Rush. However, the Dahlonega miners returned from California with new ideas of how to extract gold from the hills. Around the square of Dahlonega, businesses quickly flourished, selling everything from picks and shovels to food and lodging. A thriving town was built around the courthouse with merchants successfully growing their businesses.

1891 – North Georgia Agricultural College cadets and officers pose with their newly
acquired equipment on a hill overlooking the town.
Vanishing Georgia, Georgia Archives, University System of Georgia

History of The Smith House

The discovery of gold in 1828 caused many miners to flood the North Georgia Mountains. One of these men, James Boisclair, also known as "Free Jim," came to Dahlonega with the hopes of mining for his riches. His dream came true, he purchased many tracts of land, including the property where the Smith House sits today. He built a small structure for his living quarters, and after his death the property fell into the hands of another successful business entrepreneur.

Frank Wayland Hall

The history of the Smith House traces back to 1884, when a gentleman by the name of Captain Frank Hall purchased an acre of land east of the Dahlonega public square, formerly owned by Free Jim, to build a "Grand House." Captain Hall moved from Vermont to Dahlonega in 1868 after the Civil War. He served as a representative of The Boston Massachusetts Company to oversee local gold mills and machinery of the Dahlonega mines. Hall's fortune came from the many tracts of land he acquired, as well as a general merchandise store on the public square, Frank W Hall Merchandise Company. The Hall Block where the store was located is still visible today with the Hall name shown on top. The building next to the Hall Block is known as the Hall House, where Frank and his first wife lived and hosted many out-of-town guests. After her passing, Frank married Ester Caroline Brown and planned construction of the grand house on the plot of land he acquired previously, east of the square in 1895. During construction, workers discovered gold and quartz veins under the building. Hall validated the vein and contacted the city fathers, requesting temporary mining rights. They refused to issue rights due to concerns that the loud machinery would disrupt businesses on the square. Frank was entering into his retirement and sold all his mining rights to the Consolidated Mining Company. The couple with their infant daughter lived in the house for a short time. Shortly after construction on the home was complete, he died of typhoid fever at the age of 52 in 1901.

In 1922, Henry and Bessie Smith purchased the Hall property and opened a boarding house for hungry guests and travelers. They converted the seven rooms to accommodate guests for overnight stays, and Bessie began cooking delicious meals served on the long communal tables that we are still famous for today. Her buttermilk fried chicken, country ham, and garden fresh vegetables

Earliest known photograph of The Smith House – 1898

The Smith House c.1937

became the signature foods of the Smith House. Fame of her cooking quickly spread, and people traveled to Dahlonega to experience the Smith's hospitality. At that time, the price of a room and meal was $1.50 a day.

In 1944, William and his wife, Mary Lou, Smith moved to Dahlonega and purchased the Smith House. They wanted to open a school to educate the Appalachian children. They only lived in the home for two years before moving northward toward their school, Fort Smith Academy.

In 1946, W. B. and Effie Kate Fry purchased the property from the Smiths. They contacted Fred and Thelma Welch to run the restaurant operations. Shortly afterwards, the Welch family moved the dining operations to the basement of the original house. They had heard of the mystery of the mine shaft located under the building. Not knowing the exact location, the Frys and Welches did not realize that they were serving meals right on top of the hidden mine shaft under the basement floor. The shaft was previously boarded up by past owners, with concrete poured over it. Thelma Welch began introducing new dishes to the menu, alongside with the recipes handed down from former owners. People traveled from all over the country and the world to sample her food. Many would say they waited up to three hours on any given Sunday to feast at her table.

Henry (Ben) Smith Family

In 1970, the Frys wanted to retire from operations and offered the Welch family to purchase the property. Freddy Welch immediately started expanding the operations his parents, Fred and Thelma, had established, and creating larger dining spaces and bigger kitchens. The business grew with the help of his wife, Shirley, and after the expansions they could serve up to 2000 people on a given day. Freddy's parents retired from ownership in 1980, but his father continued to work in the business until his death. The Welch family is still continuing in the southern traditions passed down from former generations.

Fred, Thelma and young Freddy Welch

Today, the Smith House is the oldest surviving business in Dahlonega that stands in the same location. The business is still growing and expanding into different markets. The Welch family currently has the second, third, and fourth generations actively working in the business. Chris and Freida, of the third generation, have worked in the family business all of their lives and are bringing the business into the next phase of operations.

The Welch Family: Freddy, Shirley, Chris and Freida

History of the Smith House Mine Shaft

Mining most veins require the digging of a shaft and tunnels. The recommended size of a tunnel was seven square feet, which allowed several miners to be below the earth at one time. However, smaller shafts between three and four feet were common and secretly mined. When the tunnel was dug, miners placed timbers inside to keep the shaft from caving in. Sometimes the tunnels went below the water table, making it harder for the miners to work. They used pumps or barrels to clear the water, and sometimes frustrated miners abandoned the mine due to the labor required when hitting the water. The average mine depth was 20-30 feet, and the further down the shaft went, the richer the gold was. Southern gold is said to be the finest in the world. Normally, gold is 70 percent pure. Southern gold measures between 90-95 percent free of impurities. The Auraria gold constantly measured in at 95 percent. One certain account from a gold field in Dahlonega, measured a gold nugget at 99.4 percent.

Side notches where miners put boards to go down into the shaft. Wood boards were placed for easy access.

Gold Fever

"It's kind of a fever I think that kinda gets you, do it a little bit and then it grabs you – one more pan then I'm gonna find it. I think it's the fever that gets you and that's why people come here with high hopes," said Sallie Sorohan, local historian, in the Smith House video.

The Smith House Gold Mine

Captain Frank Hall built the house in 1899, and upon completion he discovered in the basement of his home a vein of gold. He was experienced in locating veins and knew this was one to investigate. However, the forefathers of Dahlonega did not want to disrupt business on the public square with heavy equipment and the noise made, so they denied his request. Sometime before 1946 the shaft was covered with concrete, with no known date of closure.

The hidden gold mine was rediscovered on February 14, 2006 in the basement of the Smith House. The location of the found mine is in the original dining room that Fred and Thelma Welch served in during the 1950s. Freddy Welch, their son, was renovating the dining room to put a lobby and restrooms for their guests.

Mike Bafile is lowered into the mine.

Workers that day were excavating the concrete floor and punched through a large opening that led to a mine shaft some twenty feet down. Immediately they removed loose dirt, finding souvenirs from the days past. Today, the dimensions of the shaft are four feet wide and thirty feet deep.

When uncovering the mine shaft, many personal belongings of previous owners and guests of the home were found. Mike Bafile, the Welch's son-in-law, was the first to be lowered into the dark shaft that had been covered for over a century. Loose dirt prompted him to start digging to see what laid underneath. "We found veins of numerous quartz rocks that appear to be rich in gold," Freddy Welch declared to the vast numbers of newspaper journalists who soon appeared wanted the headline story.

The Dahlonega Nugget

"The Gold of the News"

Volume 116, No. 49 — Wednesday, February 15, 2006 — USPS 141400

Gold mine found under The Smith House

Vein of truth in local lore

By Miriam Austin
The Nugget

Father Freddy, left, and son Chris Welch are ecstatic about the discovery of a mine below The Smith House. They frequently find old newspapers, toys, and other unusual objects buried in the walls and floors of The Smith House.

The shaft beneath the floor of The Smith House's dining room decends approximately 20 feet straight down. Based on shadows thrown by lowered lamps, the shaft appears to widen out into a larger cavern beneath the earth. Video was also taken of the mine by lowering a camera into the shaft; the footage appears to confirm the existence of a larger cavern, and also to show two separate and partially caved-in tunnels leading away, though that is yet be confirmed. (Staff photos/MIRIAM AUSTIN)

Gold in these hills? Bet The Smith House on it.

Rumors about old gold mines below the Public Square have circulated for years.

Anne Amerson, a member of the Lumpkin County Historical Society and author of many local history books, says, "One of the most popular stories is that The Smith House is sitting on a rich gold vein. Captain Hall was excavating it, so the story goes, and then he covered it back up."

According to Amerson, no one knows for sure why a life-long gold miner would cover the mine, and there was no evidence of its existence.

The rumor apparently started with a news item in the Nov. 3, 1899, edition of The Dahlonega Nugget.

The article stated: "Capt. Hall's workmen while excavating the cellar for his new ware house on the corner of Chestatee and Water streets ... struck a rich gold bearing vein several

See Discovery, Page 11A

Gold mine discovery under The Smith House 'an amazing find'

TIMELINE

1868: Frank Wayland Hall moves to Dahlonega to work as a mining superintendent. Hall's name became associated with many mines around Dahlonega.

1895: Frank Hall purchases the property where the current Smith House sits.

Nov. 3, 1899: The Dahlonega Nugget reports "Capt. Hall's workmen while excavating the cellar for his new warehouse on the corner of Chestatee and Water streets ... struck a rich gold bearing vein several feet wide, depth not known." Rumors claim that Hall reluctantly covered his gold vein with the Smith House, because the city fathers would not allow him to mine so close to the square.

May 1900: Hall moves into his new offices, now known as The Smith House, which was used as an assay office for testing gold.

Early 1910s: Hall moves away, and according to Freddy Welch, "the Smith House sat empty for 10 or 12 years."

1922: H.B. and Bessie Smith open "The Smith House Restaurant."

1946: William B. Fry, son of a gold miner and amateur prospector himself, purchases The Smith House block.

1970: Fred and Freddy Welch, father and son and long-time employees of the Frys, purchase The Smith House.

2006: The Welch family begins major renovations to the Smith House, including tearing out the dining room floor to make room for new bathrooms.

Feb. 12, 2006: A worker, chipping away at concrete, punches through the floor of the dining room into a hole. Upon further excavation, it is determined the hole is in fact a deep mining shaft, leading to underground tunnels and mines. The Welches suspect it is in fact the rumored rich gold-bearing vein Frank Hall found more than a century ago.

Continued from Page 1A

feet wide, depth not known."

The legend, it turns out, had a nugget of truth.

This past Sunday, during renovations to The Smith House's dining room, a worker punched through the concrete floor to a hole underneath.

After clearing away more concrete, Freddy Welch, owner of the establishment, discovered it was not just a hole, but a vertical mine shaft leading approximately 20 feet straight down.

With a light and a video camera lowered down the shaft, Welch determined there were two tunnels diverging from the bottom of the shaft.

One, according to Welch, appears to lead directly toward the Gold Museum — which may put to rest another rumor.

"It might confirm rumors of a shaft under the Gold Museum," Welch says.

The mine shaft itself has been sealed off since at least 1899, when Frank Hall completed his new building to be used — ironically — as an assay office for testing gold.

The newly uncovered shaft is dry, in spite of the natural springs in the area, and century-old footprints can be seen in the walls, where it appears a spelunker in the past climbed down using a rope.

As soon as the area is secure, Freddy Welch intends to be the first to follow that past spelunker's footsteps down the shaft.

Welch suspects that the story of the mine just got lost over time.

Hall built the house that covered over the mine, and then he moved in the early 1900s.

"The house sat empty 10 to 12 years before Smith bought it, and Hall was dead by then," Welch says.

The proof positive that The Smith House is literally sitting on a gold mine is beyond exciting for the Welch family.

Chris Welch, Freddy's son and the hotel manager, had just gotten off a plane when his phone rang.

"My dad was calling, and he kept telling me 'We found the gold mine! We found the gold mine!'"

It took a few minutes for Chris to realize the full impact of what his father was telling him.

He rushed home, and the pair have been determining the best course of action ever since.

The Welch family is in the middle of renovations to The Smith House. The large-scale project includes expanding the dining room, adding bathrooms, and adding another 50 rooms to the hotel. Of course "plans have changed a bit," says Chris Welch.

While renovations will continue, the first priority for the Welches is preserving this important find for Dahlonega.

They have a wealth of ideas already, from tours to lighting the mine and covering it with a glass sheet, so visitors can see it. They have discussed lining up mirrors periscope-style so that visitors can see down into the mine without having to descend.

No decisions have been made yet, and will not be until the area is secure and they can examine the find firsthand.

One thing is certain: both father and son have a very personal connection to the discovery and its implications.

Chris Welch thinks of all that history, buried there for a century, and says, "I think it's funny because I think of all the people who have sat in this dining room, right over this mine shaft."

Welch has pictures on file of people sitting at the table directly in front of the window where the mine shaft lies; his parents, his family, and even guests as esteemed as Jimmy and Rosalynn Carter.

"The staff sang happy birthday to Rosalynn in this room," he says.

Freddy Welch thinks of Bill Fry, who owned The Smith House when Freddy was a child. Bill Fry was the son of a miner, and an amateur prospector himself.

Freddy's parents worked for Fry, and Freddy grew up at The Smith House.

"He used to take us all around town, to different mines and streams," Freddy says.

"And all this time the mine was under the hotel. If he knew about this, he would flip."

One thing everyone agrees on, from the Welches to Anne Amerson to workers gathered around the hole: "It's exciting," they all say. "It's an amazing find."

Freddy contacted the Consolidated Gold Mine in Dahlonega to test the rocks, and miner Mike Clark, an expert in locating veins, ventured into the shaft to look at the vein. After taking samples back to the Consolidated Mine for testing, the test revealed the vein held a type of gold referred to as "Red Gold" because of its rich mineral composition. Clark confirmed the size and location of the vein and that the Smith House has a rich vein that travels under the main house. "The Smith House had been sitting on top of a gold mine all along," stated Miner Mike.

Smith House Vein of GOLD!

Miner Mike

Discovery of gold mine confirms old rumor

Drew Murphy

SIGHTS AND SOUNDS

The headline streams across the front page of "The Dahlonega Nugget:"

"Gold mine found under The Smith House."

I'm sure many of you have traveled through north Georgia and probably stopped or stayed at Dahlonega's historic old Smith House.

Do you remember sitting at a long table with a dozen others while platters and bowls of fried chicken, mashed potatoes and gravy, cornbread and greens were brought in from the kitchen?

I particularly recall the aroma of freshly baked yeast rolls. No dessert was served the last time I was there. We were too full.

Of course, we had no idea a gold mine had been hidden under our feet since 1899. Neither did Jimmy and Rosalynn Carter when they celebrated Rosalynn's birthday there some years back.

The old gold mine was discovered last month — Feb. 12, to be exact — when a worker punched through the dining room floor and found a large hole that led to a mine shaft 20 feet straight down.

An old rumor that The Smith House sits on a rich vein of gold was confirmed.

The thrilled owners, father and son Fred and Freddie Welch, are waiting for some soil stabilization before they descend into the dry shaft.

Renovations also are under way at the restaurant and hotel that will add new bathrooms, an expanded dining room and 50 more rooms to the hotel.

This is all reported in the charmingly local "Dahlonega Nugget" newspaper, appropriately named at its origin in the late 19th century because of the area's fame as a gold mining area.

A copy of the Feb. 5 issue of the paper was given to me by a visiting longtime Dahlonega friend, Annette Seymour. Recently widowed, Annette works part time at the town's Gold Museum. She told me a nine-piece set of gold coins minted in Dahlonega between 1838 and 1861 recently sold for $7 million. A similar set is owned by the museum.

Some other historic tidbits: A government mint once operated in Dahlonega. Mining began in the area in 1829, and the town square and its county courthouse were dedicated in 1833.

According to another newspaper, "The Times" of Gainesville, Ga., a "gold rush of 1828 brought 15,000 hopeful miners to Dahlonega between 1838 and 1861. Some $6 million in gold was coined at the U.S. Branch Mint in Dahlonega."

Many miners left the Dahlonega area after gold was discovered in 1848 at Sutter's Mill in California, prompting the largest gold rush in U.S. history.

Small-scale mining still continues in the Dahlonega area. The dome of the Georgia capitol building in Atlanta is covered in gold leaf from Dahlonega. You may have noticed it as your plane flew overhead.

My late brother Bill once owned a mountain retreat near Dahlonega. A wonderful old mountain man, known to us as Mr. Dollar, lived at the foot of the hill and looked after the place. He never showed us a secret spring where he sometimes panned for gold, but he did tell us he usually came up with about $16 worth of the ore each time.

Dahlonega still celebrates its heritage with a "Gold Rush Day" every fall. Back in the 1940s there were hog-calling and climbing-the-greased-pole contests, as well as a parade.

I remember we were late getting to town for the festivities one Saturday morning, and I wondered aloud if we had missed the parade.

A grizzled mountaineer heard me. With a smile, he turned around and said, "Yep, and they've done clumb the pole."

You may well wonder why the mine under The Smith House had been covered all these years.

One legend goes this way: When the house was built by Capt. Frank Hall in 1884, the city wouldn't permit him to dig for gold on the property, partly because it was too close to the downtown square and because he was a Yankee.

It would appear that he built the house to cover his digging. His health then failed and he sold the house and land to Henry and Bessie Smith in 1922. The property has changed hands a few times since then.

Daytona Beach News Journal the publishing date is March 12, 2006 on page 3G

Articles found in the Mine Shaft

The mine shaft rediscovered by Freddy Welch in 2006 revealed many interesting articles from days past. When the concrete that hid the shaft was removed and a deep opening was revealed, he sent light into the darkness, and only loose dirt was visible. Immediately he started digging down the shaft, bringing up loose dirt in buckets. Upon inspecting the dirt, Welch found broken pieces of china. Further digging led to items such as whiskey bottles, a medicine vile, canning jar, a light bulb, and quartz rocks. The mystery hole not only held gold, but also insightful artifacts that helped compose the past.

First sight of mine shaft when removing the concrete floor

Mike Bafile, the Welch's son-in law, dug into the loose dirt in the shaft, and when pieces of china were revealed, he started to see that there was more to the shaft than dirt. The ground was uneven. He quickly focused on what was under his feet, and realized that he was not standing on the shaft's floor. Being very careful not to fall through, since he did not know what kind of floor he was standing on, Mike tied himself off while workers held him while he explored the mine. Mike's brother, Stan, watched to make sure of his safety and inspected the items brought out of the shaft. Later, a cage was built to lower Mike down in the shaft.

Medicine vials and other health items found in shaft

Many old newspaper articles were uncovered between layers of dirt, and it seems that the papers were neatly placed to cover something underneath. Some of the papers were not readable, but there was one that possibly states the time of shaft closure. Another clue was an article found containing an interview with Ben Smith, owner from 1922-1944. He stated in an interview in *The Dahlonega Nugget* how he did not disturb the mine. William Smith owned the home in 1944, and in 1946 wanted to sell knowing that a finished basement would bring in a sizable price. Being a lawyer, he probably knew nothing about mining, and knowing there was a hole in his basement might have caused concern for his safety. Perhaps he poured the concrete floor in the basement and thus hid the mine shaft for over 60 years. When Fred and Thelma Welch moved the dining operations to the basement, they had no idea about the location of the shaft, or that they were serving meals on top of a gold mine.

Bessie Smith china collection

The broken china was soon revealed to be from Ms. Bessie Smith's serving collection. Unfortunately, most items were broken but pieces were salvaged and put back into the set. The descendants of the Smith family were at the Smith House soon after the discovery and validated the pieces as part of Bessie's collection. Annie Laurie Smith, granddaughter to Bessie, remembered her serving from the dishes while on her visits. Silverware was found that was used in serving her boarding customers. Her family also authenticated that the medicine bottles found in the shaft were used by Bessie to give herself shots for diabetes. Another interesting artifact is the initialed lotion case belonging to Frank Hall's mother, Marianda Hall. Mrs. Hall probably lived at the Smith House in one of the upstairs rooms. There were other jars found that were used for creams and medical remedies. These jars are thought to be Marianda's because of the age of the jars, and some of the jars found still had the original contents in it.

Also found were many glass bottles of different types of whiskey. One in particular is a square-shaped Johnnie Walker whiskey bottle, which is a Scotch whiskey dating from the late 19th century. The marking on the jar is John Walker and Son, and the square bottle was introduced to the market in the 1870s. The company name was changed to Johnnie Walker shortly after the square bottles were introduced. The actual date of this jar is believed to date between the 1870-1880s.

Johnnie Walker and Son whisky

Digging of the shaft reached down to the water table. Surprisingly, a light bulb emerged from the water. It was identified as a GE Mazda light bulb manufactured in 1909. Amazingly, when placed in a modern lamp, the light bulb still worked. GE was contacted, and they confirmed the authenticity of this bulb as one of their own. They wrote an article in the Consumer & Industrial News about the discovery:

"At the site of an old gold mine shaft, underneath the Smith House Inn in Dahlonega, Georgia, workers uncovered a GE Mazda tungsten light bulb. Much to their surprise, the lamp still burns being nearly 100 years." May 15, 2007

Other finds included: an old corn whiskey jar (used in the 1880s to transport corn liquor by means of the river), a LE Jung New Orleans jar (storing of absinthe), an Ancient Age whiskey bottle, old Blue Plate mayonnaise jar, Atlas EZ seal canning jar, as well as jars used for different purposes.

GE Mazda light bulb

Of course, the most prominent finding was gold! Mike was so amazed by the items he found in the shaft that he overlooked the vein right in front of him. Descending into the shaft one more time, he saw a formation coming out of the side of the wall. Using a pick, he cleaned around the rock formation and found the true treasure: the gold vein running under the building.

Corn Whisky jar, LE Jung jar, Ancient Age whiskey, Blue Plate Mayo, EZ canning jar

Currently, all of the artifacts we have salvaged are on display in front of the mine shaft in the lower level of the Smith House.

Smith House Museum

(left) Miner Mike in the Smith House DVD playing on the television screen behind the glass of the mineshaft display explaining the miner's technique of extracting gold.

Artifacts found in Mine Shaft

Entrance to the Smith House mine shaft

The Smith House DVD

As soon as Freddy realized that this was truly the legendary mine shaft of Frank Hall, he called Video Craft Production to produce a video about the mine and its history. The "Legend of the Smith House Mine" hosts past owners of the Smith House, interviewing them about their time spent at the home, as well as a local historian who shares facts about the development of Dahlonega. The video won two bronze Telly Awards from the film industry.

An excerpt from a local newspaper described the documentary as such: "A video chronicling the gold mine under the Dahlonega's historic Smith House has captured two awards for video production. 'Legend of the Smith House Mine' was awarded two bronze Telly Awards in both the TV documentary and low budget categories. The annual awards honors the best in local, regional, and cable television commercials and programs, as well as video and film productions and work created for the web. The winning video was produced by Scott and Sherry Gray, owners of Video Craft Production. 'The Legend of the Smith House Mine' documentary DVD features the legend and reality of the gold mine beneath the Smith House Inn."

Film crew videoing with workers

Aurora Award

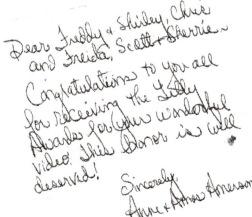

Behind the Scenes: Making the DVD

Right: Mike Bafile takes part in the filming.

Family Style Dining

Family Style Definition
Family style dining is a meal served to a group of people who are not necessarily related, seated together at one table with platters of food which are passed around "family style."

Family Style Dining Design
All food is brought to the table on platters and in bowls with serving spoons and tongs. The food is passed around the table for guests to serve themselves what they like and take how much they want. Then there is the interaction as someone says, "Please pass the potatoes." The design is to put people at their ease, and help them feel at home. Friendships are sometimes formed, and most people love it.

Etiquette of Family Style Service
- Serve food with left hand from guest's left.
- Beverages served from right hand from guest's right shoulder.
- Serve women first (oldest to youngest), then children, and last men.
- Position plates attractively with main dishes in front of guests.
- Ask guest before refilling glasses or dishes.
- Guest moving knife and/or fork to the top of plate indicate they are finished and ready for plate to be removed from table.
- Clear all dishes when guests are finished with right hand and from right side of guest.
- When all plates are removed from table, offer hot beverages before desserts are served.

Smith House Family Style Dining 1960s

Advantages of Family Style Dining for Children

- All food is served on table encouraging group socialization.
- A beverage such as tea, juice, and water is set with dinner.
- They are encouraged to try new foods and second portions.

Family Style Guest Instruction

- All dishes are set on table at same time.
- All members serve themselves from the dishes on tables.
- Adults serve those who are not able to serve themselves.
- Adults are to encourage group participation and supervise amount of food consumed by members.
- Refill of the bowls are the members responsibility to ask for seconds.
- Conversation after dinner is mandatory.

The Smith House

Earliest known photograph of the Smith House – 1898

Salads and Soups

Tomato: A fruit or vegetable?

The tomato originated in Mexico, and was spread to the United States by the Spanish explorers in the early 18th century. To figure out if a tomato is a fruit or a vegetable, you need to know what makes it a fruit. The definition of a fruit is "a plant with seeds," of which tomatoes have more than enough. However, in most dishes, excluding salads and sandwiches, tomatoes are considered the prime vegetable ingredient. Recipes such as tomato sauces, vegetable soup, and ketchup are a few examples where most people identify the tomato to be a vegetable. The answer to the question is that a tomato is technically the fruit of the tomato plant, but it is used as a vegetable in cooking.

When the Spanish explorer Hernando De Soto led an expedition through this region in 1540, he visited a Cherokee village at Nacoochee. The Cherokee Indians appeared to have been settled in the area for a very long time. Could De Soto have brought with him the delicate tomato and introduced the fruit to the Indian population?

In 1837, the *Gazetter of Georgia* had a segment about the finding of the ancient Indian village in the Nacoochee Valley:

> "In 1834, a subterranean Indian Village was discovered in Nacoochee Valley, in Georgia, by gold miners, whilst excavating a canal for the purpose of washing gold. The depth of which it is covered varies from seven to nine feet; some of the houses are embedded in a stratum of rich auriferous gravel. There are thirty-four in number, built of logs, from six to ten inches in diameter, and from ten to twelve feet in length. The walls are from three to six feet in height; forming a continuous line or street of three hundred feet. The logs are hewn and notched as at the present day. The land, beneath which they were found, was covered, at the first settlement by the whites, with a heavy growth of timber, denoting the great antiquity of those buildings, and a powerful cause which submerged them. Cane baskets and fragments of earthenware were found in the rooms; the houses are situated from fifty to a hundred yards from the principal channel of the creek. A great number of curious specimens of workmanship have been found in situations which preclude the possibility of their having been moved for more than a thousand years."

DAHLONEGA "CITY OF GOLD"

When Hernando De Soto forged through the Lumpkin County area in search of "El Dorado," "The City of Gold," little did he dream how close it was. Three hundred years later and 20 years before the California Gold Rush, gold was struck in Dahlonega in 1828 by Benjamin Parks, and the first major American Gold Rush was on.

Today, prospectors still come to Dahlonega and Lumpkin County in search of gold and find much more! Like the warm, southern hospitality that abounds here, making everyone feel welcome.

On the public square, which is listed in The National Register, quaint and interesting shops offer a myriad of outstanding wares, including many that are locally created. A variety of cuisines can also be found in Dahlonega's fine restaurants, including southern cooking at its best.

The home of North Georgia College, founded in 1873, Dahlonega and Lumpkin County offer to visitors a place for year-round enjoyment and activities. Ideally situated within the North Georgia mountains and only fifty miles from metro Atlanta, the more than 14,000 residents here will tell you Dahlonega is truly an "El Dorado" ... a gem of a place!

"TALONEGA"
Cherokee word for yellow metal

Smith House Summer Salad

6 tomatoes
2 cucumbers
1 onion

Dressing
4 ounces of white vinegar
4 ounces of water
1 pack of dry Italian dressing mix
1 tablespoon olive oil

Wash and cut all vegetables into cube-size portions. Mix the liquids together and pour over vegetables. May add a teaspoon of sugar if the dressing is tart. Let salad sit in fridge for one hour. Salad can be served on top of lettuce.

Smith House Cabbage Salad

1 heads of cabbage, chopped
½ onion, chopped
1 cups of sliced carrots
1 large cucumber cubed

Dressing
1 package of Hidden Valley spices and herb dressing
1 cup white vinegar
⅓ cup sugar optional
⅓ cup of vegetable or olive oil

Mix cabbage, onion, carrots, and cucumbers. In a separate bowl, mix all dressing ingredients together and stir thoroughly. Pour over cabbage and toss.

Smith House Coleslaw

1 heads of cabbage
1 carrot
¼ of an onion
½ green pepper

Dressing
1 cup sugar
½ cup white vinegar
2 cups of mayonnaise
¼ cup of milk
1 teaspoon salt
1 teaspoon pepper
2 tablespoons celery seeds optional

In a food processor, chop cabbage & carrot together. Empty and then chop onion and green pepper. Combine chopped vegetables together in a glass bowl. In a separate bowl, mix vinegar, mayonnaise, salt & pepper, sugar, and celery seed. Pour over cabbage and mix until coated. Store in refrigerator for one hour before serving.

The Three Sisters

The Holy Trinity in the culinary world is simply a combination of three starter ingredients to most dishes in many cultures. To the Cherokee Indians, corn, beans, and squash make up their Holy Trinity, which is also known as the "Three Sisters." The first sister is the bean. Beans have vines that need tall poles to grow on and are planted next to the second sister, the corn. Corn is a tall stalk that serves as the tall pole for the bean vine. The vine, in return, brings nitrogen to the soil that the corn needs for survival. The third sister is the squash. Squash is planted between the rows of corn, and the squash serves as a perfect ground cover to keep the weeds away. The squash leaves provide shade from the hot sun to protect the shallow roots of the corn plant.

Cooking usually consisted of the three items plus a wild meat. Traditionally, the Cherokee ate one-course meals, without separate courses such as appetizers or desserts. The Indians ate food that was simply prepared, food that they hunted or gathered. They ate two main meals a day. In the morning they had cornmeal mush, or cereal. Corn was an important snack between meals. The Cherokee also would eat this in the evening, with meat and vegetable stew, broiled meat, or fish. Usually a dinner table would consist of wild meat, a "three sister dish," pumpkins, and dried fruit. Fruits were simply dried from the sun. The Cherokee built a scaffold from poles out in the yard and placed the fruit, which they cut into small pieces, out in the sun until they dried. The fruit was then sacked and stored up in the lofts of their homes. Sweet potatoes were a root vegetable that was common food because it was easy for them to cultivate yearly. During the winter months, plenty of wild meats were stored including deer, turkey, squirrels, and other small animals. Hogs were in abundant supply and ran wild over the hills, usually all throughout the year. Canning was not a method people used for storage in the early years, as that technology and materials were not yet present. Usually, meats and fruits were always dried. Hospitality was always important among the Cherokee tribe, and guests were always served first at meals.

Courtesy of the New York State Museum

Three Sisters Salad

- 1 can black or kidney beans (rinsed and drained)
- 1 cup frozen corn (thawed and drained)
- 2 medium squash or zucchini
- ½ red onion
- 1 bag of romaine lettuce
- Fresh parmesan cheese

Dressing
- 2 tablespoons fresh lemon juice
- ½ teaspoon sea salt
- 1 tablespoon red wine vinegar
- ¼ cup olive oil
- ¼ tablespoon ground black pepper

Whisk the dressing ingredients together in a small bowl and set aside. Wash vegetables and lettuce. Cut squash and onions in bite-size pieces. Tear or chop the romaine lettuce into medium-sized pieces. In a large bowl, mix vegetables, lettuce, and beans together and toss in dressing. Top with desired amount of parmesan cheese.

Cranberry Salad

- 3- 8 ounce packages of cranberries washed and de-stemmed
- 1- 3 ounce package strawberry flavored gelatin
- 1 cup sugar
- 1 cup of boiling water
- 1 teaspoon cinnamon
- 1 tablespoon lemon juice
- 1 apple and 1 orange (peeled & cored) finely ground
- 1 can crushed pineapple, drained
- 1 cup chopped celery
- 1 cup chopped walnuts

In a food processor, grind cranberries, apples, and oranges. Boil water and add gelatin. Add sugar and cinnamon to the gelatin, stirring until dissolved. Empty processor into a bowl and add lemon juice and celery. Drain pineapple juice and add to cranberry mixture. Stir mixture gently then pour into a large casserole dish and chill overnight.

Strawberry or Blueberry Salad **Plan ahead***

- 1 large package frozen strawberries or blueberries
- 1- 6 ounce package strawberry-flavored gelatin
- 1 small can crushed pineapple with juice
- 2 cups boiling water
- 1- 8 ounce package cream cheese
- 1 cup sour cream
- 1 cup sugar
- ½ teaspoon vanilla
- Pecans or walnuts, chopped

Drain pineapple and reserve juice. Dissolve gelatin in boiling water and add the reserved juice. In the bottom of a glass casserole dish, layer strawberries, pineapple, and gelatin mix and refrigerate overnight. Combine sour cream, cream cheese, sugar, vanilla, and beat until smooth. Pour evenly over gelatin when firm. Sprinkle nuts to garnish.

The Famous who dined at The Smith House: Remembered by Doris Abee

Doris Abee started working at the Smith House in 1952 when she was 14 years old. She learned how to cook under Fred Riley, the head cook at that time. He taught her how to make most of the traditional recipes handed down from Bessie Smith (owner 1922-1946), as well as pies and salads. One time, she ran out of mayonnaise and substituted it with mustard without telling the cooks. Doris stumbled onto a new recipe, the "Lettuce and Boiled Egg Salad," which was published in the June 1963 Ford Times alongside a painting of the Smith House (page 51). Other recipes were sent to the Times, and they picked the "Macaroni and Cheese Casserole" recipe. They called Doris up from Detroit, Michigan to ask questions about dishes.

Doris had the pleasure to serve Jimmy Carter (while he was running for governor), Lester Maddox, Tip O'Neil, General Westmoreland, and Dr. Charles Allen, who was in Dahlonega for a week talking to students at the college. Bob Hope was in Dahlonega after attending a golf tournament in Augusta in the 1970s and visited the Smith House. He bragged over all the food served, especially the fried chicken, yeast rolls, and candied yams. He was friendly and cracked a lot of jokes, just like he did on TV, Doris recalled. Mr. Hope signed his autograph on his guest check for her. This was during an election year, and he made a bet with someone that Nixon was going to win- and he did.

Pat Nixon, Richard's twin brother, also ate at the restaurant. He liked Doris' party salad so much that he requested a copy of the recipe to be sent to the White House. Doris received a nice letter from Mrs. Nixon on White House stationary dated October 27, 1973, saying "I deeply appreciate your thoughtfulness in sending a copy of your recipe for 'Abee Salad.' The considerate friendship your kind sharing represents is truly meaningful."

Ford Times, June 1963

Smith House Abee Apple Salad

- 3 packages lime-flavored gelatin (can use sugar-free)
- 3 cups hot water
- 30 mini marshmallows
- 1- 8 ounce package cream cheese
- 1 small can crushed pineapple
- 1 cup whipped cream
- ½ cup mayonnaise
- 1 cup chopped pecans

Dissolve gelatin in hot water and stir. Cool slightly before adding cream cheese. Set aside to stiffen. Just before it has congealed, whip with a rotary beater until smooth. Add pineapple, mayonnaise, and whipped cream. In a large glass casserole dish, split marshmallows in half and add pecans. Pour mix over marshmallows and chill until set. Cherries may be added for variation.

Lettuce and Boiled Egg Salad

From the *Ford Times* June 1963 magazine

- ½ head of lettuce, broken in pieces
- 1 medium onions, sliced in thin rings
- 6 hard-boiled eggs, sliced

Dressing

- ½ cup mayonnaise
- 1 tablespoon mustard
- 2 tablespoons white vinegar
- 1 teaspoon salt
- 1 teaspoon black pepper

Combine lettuce, onions, and eggs in a salad bowl. Mix dressing ingredients in a separate bowl. Pour mixture over lettuce and toss.

Apple-Pineapple Slaw

- 3 cups shredded cabbage
- 1 (9 ounce) can pineapple tidbits, drained
- 1 cup diced apples (peeled and cored)
- ½ cup chopped celery
- 1 cup tiny marshmallows

Dressing

- ½ cup mayonnaise
- 1 teaspoon of lemon juice

Wash cabbage removing outer leaves and cut into ¼ pieces and process in a food processor. Wash apples and celery. Cut celery into ¼ pieces. In a large mixing bowl, add shredded cabbage, pineapples, celery, and apple. Coat ingredients with dressing and stir well. Fold in marshmallows. Chill before serving.

Sequoya's Alphabet

The Indians called him Sikwayi, but the white man found the pronunciation of his name too difficult and called him Sequoya. His mother was a Cherokee Native American and his father, a white man. The Cherokee Alphabet was invented in 1821 and had an immediate influence on the Cherokees. It seems that a group of young Indian men discussed the points at which they and white people excelled. They praised the agility of the Indian, his fleetness of foot, the accuracy with which he aimed his arrows, and his great physical endurance. However, all were deeply impressed with the fact that the white man could "put talk on paper," and how it could be understood in faraway lands and after a long period of time. A silent member of the group, Sequoya, said that he also could find a way to "put talk on paper." Upon saying this, he picked up a flat rock and scratched on it a few symbols, which he pretended to read.

Sequoya produced an alphabet of eighty-six characters; the English alphabet only has twenty-six characters. However, there are many sounds in the Cherokee Alphabet for which English has no single character. The Cherokee devised a character for each of these sounds. Seven years after the completion of the Cherokee Alphabet, Sequoya visited Washington and was given a donation of $500, along with an impressive award which was *"for the great benefit he conferred upon the Cherokee people, in the beneficial results which they are experiencing from the use of the alphabet discovered by him."*

The Cherokee Nation embraced Sequoya's system and became an academy for the study of the Alphabet. Younger students also learned the English language along with the Cherokee system of living. An active correspondence began between the eastern and western divisions. Plans were made for a national press, with a library and museum to be established at the capital, New Echota. The first issue of the Cherokee newspaper was printed on February 21, 1828 at New Echota about 75 miles west of Dahlonega. Galagina, meaning "The Buck" in Cherokee was the first editor of the paper. He was educated at a missionary school in Cornwall, Connecticut and his fellow students at the college knew him as Elias Boudinot. The paper quickly traveled to all parts of the Cherokee nations and in Dahlonega was read in wigwams and huts.

Courtesy of Georgia Archives

ABC Soup

As my grandfather, Fred Welch, grew older and started to trust my cooking, he would ask me to prepare certain dishes when he was ill. One day he had a very bad cold, so I decided to prepare a big pot of vegetable soup with every type of food available in my pantry. As my grandfather was sipping on the soup, he observed the different vegetables I had in the bowl. He proclaimed that "this soup had everything in it, including the kitchen sink!" I didn't know whether to take his comment as a compliment or not. A

A replica of an Cherokee Indian homestead in the 1800s
Courtesy of the National Archives

confirmation came a few months later when he had another cold, and grandfather asked me to fix the soup that had everything in it including the kitchen sink. We both laughed and I gladly made him a batch of the soup that we named the ABC soup.

ABC Soup

5 medium fresh tomatoes, diced or 1 can of diced tomatoes
1 32-oz. carton of chicken broth
½ pound of ground beef (turkey or chicken can be substituted)
½ onion
1 clove of garlic
Desired amount of frozen vegetables or fresh vegetables
    Okra, butter beans, corn, carrots, green peas, any other vegetable available
1 teaspoon sea salt
½ teaspoon pepper
Flavored rice or plain if desired (can use frozen rice and vegetable pack)
Vegetable seasonings to taste
Two pinches of cinnamon (optional)

In a large pot add enough olive oil to coat bottom on medium heat. Add tomatoes (if using fresh tomatoes let them steam until done with covered lid-approx. 4 minutes) and chicken broth. In a coated fry pan, brown meat until almost done and then add onions and garlic. In a separate sauce pan, cook rice until done. To the tomatoes, add desired vegetables, salt & pepper, vegetable seasoning and bring to a boil. Add rice at this point (Can use the already cooked bag of rice that includes frozen vegetables). Before serving, stir in the cinnamon if preferred. The cinnamon gives the soup a little something different that your guest can't figure out what makes it so good.

Southerners prefer to eat their soup with cornbread and a big glass of sweet tea!

New Found Friends

Benjamin Parks' family moved to the Hall County area from North Carolina when he was a young man in the early 1800s. His family lived on the east side of the Chestatee River near the Cherokee Nation. In a remote location, he started on foot playing in the vast countryside and exploring the terrain for hidden treasures. Little did he know that he would someday stumble onto treasure beyond his wildest expectations, "the discovery of gold in the North Georgia Mountains."

Parks remembered that the Indians lived all around when he came to Georgia. He noticed his neighbors being different from himself; they had dark-colored skin and braided hair with feathers. Parks wondered how they lived and wanted to explore their culture. Maybe they were big hunters since he loved going into the woods to hunt for deer. Hunting provided his family with the necessary nourishment they needed, and family gardens added plentiful vegetables to their meals. Parks would cross westward over the frontier into the Cherokee Nation to tend his cattle and horses. When venturing onto the Cherokee lands, he was welcomed by the friendly inhabitants. Over time, Parks formed lasting friendships. He shared his experiences of living in the white man's world, while the Indians shared their customs by welcoming Parks into their homes regularly. He learned their games and soon their knowledge of hunting wild prey in the extensive Cherokee forests.

The Cherokee houses were made of river cane and plaster, with thatched roofs. These dwellings were as strong and warm as log cabins. Parks delivered food prepared from his home and share in the natives' meals. His favorite dish the Indians prepared for him was also a native favorite, "Conee-Banee." Growing older, Parks continued in his visits, but they were less frequent because his interests kept him away. He started a livestock business with a friend, John Ralston, and they regularly salted with hollowed-out logs the area that is now the Dahlonega public square. The area became known as "Licklog." It was a frontier practice to "salt" the livestock by placing salt blocks in grazing areas.

Parks relayed the story of hunting near the Calhoun Mine on his birthday, October 27, 1828 on the property of Robert O'Barr, a preacher. Parks was "following a deer path northwest hoping it wouldn't turn across the river, for late October is no time for fording. I wasn't walking good as common and was well nigh tired down for I wore some new birthday boots not yet broke in. Crossing a little dried-up watercourse I kicked up a nice quartz piece with a sparkle to it that caught my eye. When I looked I knew it had to be but only one thing – gold!"

(North GA Journal Vol. 2 No. 1 Spring 1985 as told by Bob Meaders to Ben's daughter Margaret.)

Remembering the stories his Indian friends told him of the vast amount of gold in the area, Benjamin Parks realized it had now become reality. He approached Rev. O'Barr, who owned the area near Cherokee lands, and requested a lease on his property to mine gold. Doubtful, Rev. O'Barr agreed and would share in one-fourth of the gold mined. Parks went over to the spot with a pan, turning over dirt, and found rocks with a shiny, yellow tint and knew the content was gold. It was more than O'Barr could believe, and he wanted to annul the lease with Parks, who refused. He sold the 239 acres to Judge Underwood, who then sold it to Senator John C. Calhoun of South Carolina, who later became 1825-1832 Vice President of the United States from 1825-1832.

The Calhoun Mine is perhaps the oldest and best-known mine in Lumpkin County. The mine was added to the National Register of Historic Places and became a National Historic Landmark in 1973.

Conee-Banee Soup

3 pounds cut up chicken, venison, beef, or wild meat
¼ cup cooking oil
2 cloves of garlic
2 -28 ounce cans tomatoes
1½ teaspoon salt
1-10 ounce packages frozen cut corn
1-10 ounce package lima beans
2 tablespoons cornstarch
1 onions, quartered
1 bay leaf
Pinch of thyme optional
1 teaspoon pepper
⅓ cup cold water

In a frying pan, brown meat in oil and when meat is almost done add onion and garlic. In a large cooking pot, add tomatoes, meat, bay leaf, thyme, and salt & pepper. When bubbling, cover and reduce heat. Simmer for 1 hour. Add corn and lima beans and simmer again for 30 minutes more. Remove bay leaf. Dissolve cornstarch in water. Add to stew, stirring gently until thick and clear. Season to taste. Serves 8-12 portions

Hearty Beef Stew

2 pounds stew meat cut into 1½ inch cubes
¼ cup all-purpose flour
3 tablespoons vegetable or olive oil
4 cups water
1-8 ounce can tomato sauce
1-2 garlic cloves
2 teaspoon salt and ¼ teaspoon pepper
1 bay leaf
6 medium potatoes, quartered
6 medium carrots cut into 1 inch pieces
3 medium onions, quartered cut into 1 inch pieces
¼ cup cornstarch and ¼ cup of water

Biscuits
2 cups flour
⅓ cup shortening
¾ cup milk
2 teaspoons baking powder
3 teaspoons salt

In a bowl, coat meat with flour and then add to a fry pan in hot oil until meat is done. In a large cooking pot, add 4 cups water, tomato sauce, cooked meat, garlic, bay leaf, salt and pepper. Bring to a boil, and then reduce to medium heat. Cover and simmer 30 minutes (could simmer up to 1 hour) or until meat is tender. To the cooking pot, add potatoes, carrots, and onions and cover and simmer until vegetables are tender about ½ hour. Remove bay leaf. Blend cornstarch and ¼ cup water; add to stew and stir until mixture boils. Simmer 5 minutes. Place stew in large, shallow baking dish and top with biscuits. Bake 425 degree for 20-25 minutes.

Biscuits: Combine flour, baking powder and salt in bowl. Cut in shortening until mixture resembles coarse meal. Add milk and stir just enough to moisten well. Knead dough 8-10 times until lightly floured surface. Roll or pat to ½ inch thickness. Cut into 2 inch biscuits.

A Love Story Goes Wrong

As a young man, Benjamin Parks visited regularly with his Cherokee friends. He enjoyed learning the Indians' way of life. One day, as he was on his way home, he noticed a beautiful Indian woman adorned with custom-made jewelry. She was the most beautiful girl he had ever seen. As he eyed her, her body flowed with the river in the background. She finished her chores at the river and headed back home. Parks knew everyone in the village, but he didn't remember seeing her around. Suddenly aware of his awkward stare, she blushed to show she welcomed his attention. Parks, wanting to know more about this girl, headed in her direction but she was gone without a trace. He asked his native friends about her, and they finally understood what he was frantically trying to explain to them. The Indians at that time were new to the English language and later would be able to fully understand the English tongue.

The next day, Parks couldn't wait to return to find the mystery girl. He sat beside a large evergreen and waited for the girl to come down the path. She gazed passed him with an inviting smile and headed to the river for her daily chores. With shaky knees, he mustered enough courage and walked over to where she was and introduced himself. Parks used hand gestures and broken words to communicate with her. She laughed in amusement at his awkwardness, smiled and said to him, "Hello, my name is Elizabeth. You can call me Betsy. My father is the chief Indian of this tribe, and he gave me this nickname." He was both amazed at her plain English and overcome with curiosity. Why is she so fluent in her English speaking and the others very vague in their skills? She explained to him that being an Indian princess required more education and social skills to lead the tribe.

They talked about their experiences living in the North Georgia Mountains, including many stories of white men coming to the area. Betsy explained that some whites were welcomed but others they knew where there more for gold than for friendship. Natives had to defend their land not only from neighboring tribes, but also from curious Spanish explorers on expeditions. Betsy was told the stories of the Spanish conquistador Hernando De Soto and his band of explorers who came through the area in 1540. The clans were leery of their presence. She heard of a young native showing the Spaniards how gold was mined, melted, and refined by his people. The legend was that De Soto was more curious about tales of men in this area wearing golden hats, and gifts of gold being given in great quantities. Other tribes saw more and more explorers entering onto their land; they were more afraid of the foreign presence scaring away the game for food supplies.

Betsy spoke of the spinning wheels which arrived in 1792, along with cotton. The women thrived on producing and selling hand-made goods. They adapted European clothing styles, including long braided or beaded jackets, cotton blouses, full skirts decorated with ribbon appliqué, feathered turbans, and the calico tear dress.

Parks and the princess looked forward to their daily visits beside the tree at the river. Soon their friendship evolved from friendly talks into romantic feelings. Parks eventually mustered the courage to ask the Indian chief for his daughter's hand in marriage. The chief told him that in the Cherokee Nation the white man enjoyed all of the amenities and privileges of the Cherokee people, except that whites were not eligible for public office. It is said that whites preferred living in the Nation as opposed to being a residence in the United States. Men made political decisions for the tribe, while women made social decisions. The females of the tribe were elevated in status and respected. Mixed-race, to the Cherokee, meant children conceived by white mothers and Cherokee fathers. Children conceived by Cherokee mothers, regardless of the race of the father, were already accepted as part of the tribe. The men participated in hunting, war, and diplomacy. The women were in charge of farming, property, and family. National pride and a spirit of independence were the marks of Cherokee character.

Parks' Indian friends were anxious for the match, but his family did not accept it. He pondered upon the idea, but the reality seemed impossible to him. Betsy felt his distance toward her, therefore she never brought up talks about marriage again. However, Parks' friend Ralston, who accompanied some of his trips on their way to salt the animals at Licklog, did marry a Cherokee Indian and defended the nation during the Indian removal.

When word spread about Parks' discovery of gold near the Cherokee Nation, miners from several states rushed into the area. Natives saw this as an intrusion from the white people. From the view-point of Georgians, the land belonged to them and not the Indians. The United States government had an interest in the region, as the Indians were wards of the government. Several treaties existed between the United States and the Cherokee nation, and it was the purpose of the state to parcel out the lands to private owners as soon as possible. The Indians took an appeal to the United States Supreme Court. However, the law of Georgia was by legislative act extended over the Cherokee Nation, ignoring the Cherokees' own system of government and laws. The final treaty that nullified the Cherokee claims in Georgia was negotiated at New Echota and signed December 29, 1835. The principal terms of the treaty were that the Indians would surrender their lands and receive, in consideration thereof, an equivalent amount of land west of the Mississippi River, and in addition also receive $5,000,000. Many of the leading Cherokees were opposed to the treaty, and it is probable that the treaty expressed the desires of only a small minority of the Cherokees. The treaty stated that the last of the Indians must have departed no later than May 23, 1838. As that date approached, many Cherokees refused to leave, forcing the U.S. government to take further action.

Parks' Cherokees friends were removed from their lands and taken to the Auraria Station, where they waited for their westward journey to their new land promised by the U.S. He never saw his friends again and wondered what happened to the princess. Later on, Parks did marry Sally Henderson from North Carolina, and together they had ten boys and one girl.

Atlanta Journal July 15, 1894 (Moran conducting the interview with Frank Hall assisting) with Benjamin Parks and also from the book North Georgia Journal

Benjamin and Sally Parks

Parks preferred hunting and farming – the quiet life – to the excitement of gold mining. He was proud of his ability as a hunter. He lived to regret his gold discovery, feeling that he caused the area to grow too rapidly. (told by Ross McDonald)

Vanishing Georgia, Georgia Archives,
University System of Georgia

1832 Land Lottery Tickets

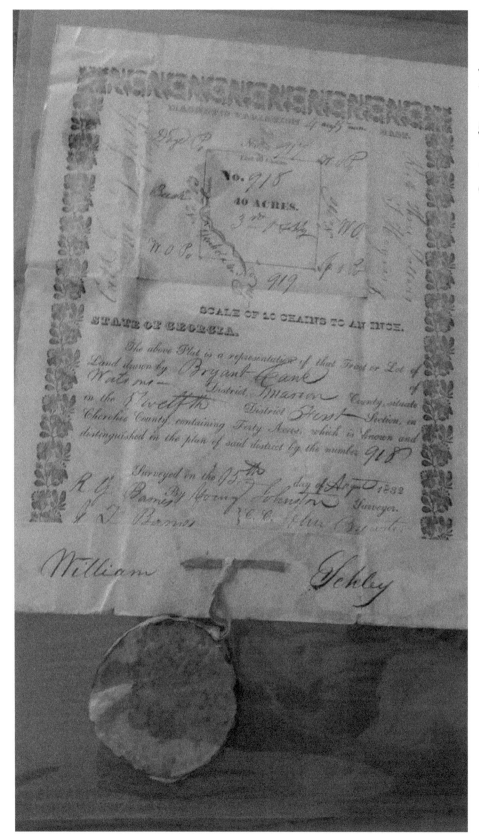

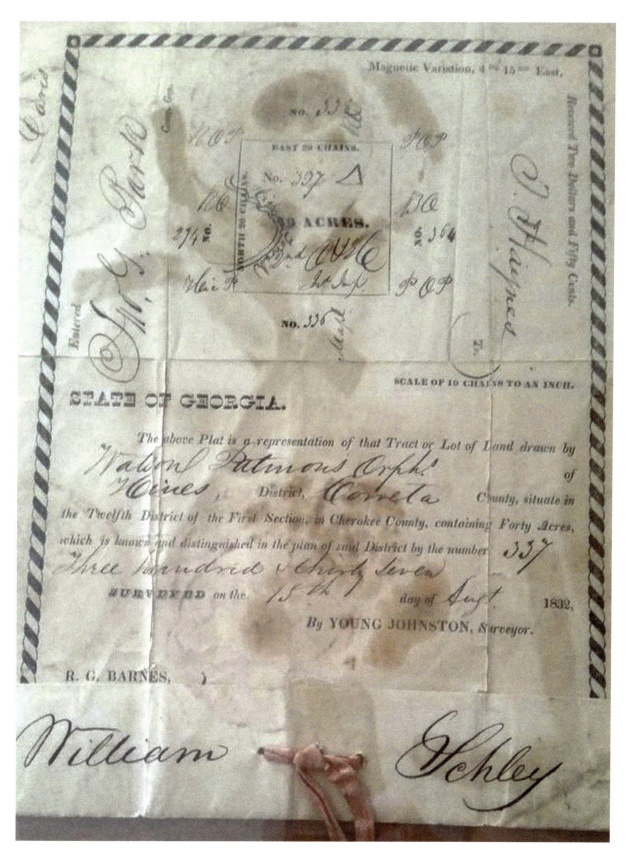

Courtesy of Jimmy Anderson

Smith House

Meats

Beginning of the Smith House

Ben & Bessie Smith, 1922

Henry Benjamin (Ben) Smith was born in Lumpkin County on July 14, 1878. He married Bessie Camilla Bowen on November 2, 1900 and had five children. Two of their grandchildren are interviewed in the Smith House DVD, sharing their experiences of visits to their grandparents at the Smith House inn and restaurant. In June of 1923, Ben and Bessie Smith purchased a home formerly owned by Captain Frank Hall. The couple began remodeling the home and converted it into a seven-room inn for travelers. Bessie, who had a passion for cooking, began preparing meals for her guests. Her recipes have been served on the Smith House's family-style tables since 1923, especially her famous fried chicken recipe. Before long, Bessie developed a restaurant operation, and her reputation for fine southern cooking quickly spread.

Her main dishes consisted of southern fried chicken, country ham that was cured on their property, and cooked vegetables, all of which were served on long communal tables. Bessie raised the chickens behind the house. Vernon Smith, her son, recalled how his mother put him in charge of taking care of the chickens she cooked for meals. Vernon caught the chickens and placed them into pens so he could fatten them up. When the chickens' size met his mother's approval, he would prepare them for dishes. To tenderize the chicken, Bessie soaked the meat in buttermilk and then dredged it in a flour mixture before frying on the wood burning stove. She did all her cooking on wood stoves. Mrs. Smith's favorite dishes to prepare were casseroles, as she grew most of the vegetables in the back yard. She also kept two cows out back to milk for daily rations.

The kitchen and dining room were located on the first floor of the main house. The inn's seven rooms were located upstairs above the dining room. Popularity quickly rose, and soon their little inn became famously known as "The Smith House." For $1.50 a day, a traveler had a room and their meals. After Bessie's death on March 9, 1939, Ben continued to run the Smith House until 1944. He sold the business to William Manning Smith, who was of no relation. Ben continued to live in the house for some time after the sale. In a 1940 newspaper article, Ben Smith describes his thoughts about the mining shaft located under the Smith House:

> *"He will tell of the vein of gold that runs under the house where they sit, discovered years ago when the basement was dug and undisturbed by him, because someday somebody will come along who needs it more than I do."*

Smith House Southern Fried Chicken

Mixture of chicken breast, thighs, legs and wings
2 cups of self-rising flour
2½ teaspoons salt
2½ teaspoons pepper
2 cups of buttermilk
Vegetable oil for deep fryer

Preheat deep fryer to 300° and add vegetable oil. Wash chicken pieces and remove skin if preferred. If the chicken breasts are large, cut into half. Turn thighs over and run finger up the bone to release the membrane. Take the thigh and fold in half to release the inner bone. In a separate bowl, combine flour, 1½ salt and 1½ pepper together. In another bowl pour the buttermilk with 1 teaspoon salt and 1 teaspoon pepper. Add chicken to soak for 3-5 minutes. Then roll the pieces in the flour mixture, shaking off the excess flour. Drop the individual pieces into the deep fryer for approximately 13-15 minutes or until done. Turn pieces after 6 minutes. Drain pieces and serve hot.

Smith House Fried Chicken Tenders

16 ounce of boneless breast strips
1 cup of buttermilk
2 cups of self-rising flour
1 teaspoon salt
1 teaspoon season salt
1 teaspoon pepper
2 cups of self-rising flour
Vegetable oil for deep fryer
Optional:
¼ teaspoon cayenne pepper
¼ teaspoon garlic
¼ teaspoon paprika

Preheat deep fryer to 300° and add vegetable oil. Wash chicken strips. In a separate bowl, combine flour, ½ teaspoon salt, ½ teaspoon pepper and ½ teaspoon season salt together. In another bowl pour the buttermilk and add the rest of the salt, pepper and season salt and stir. Add chicken strips to soak for 3-5 minutes. Then roll the pieces in the flour mixture, shaking off the excess flour. Drop the individual pieces into the fryer for approximately 7-9 minutes or until done. Turn once half way through cooking time.

Buttermilk Baked Chicken

Mixture of breast, thighs, and legs
1 tablespoon butter or margarine
¾ cup buttermilk
¾ cup flour
1½ tsp salt and pepper
¼ cup butter or margarine
1 (10.5 ounce) can cream of chicken soup

Preheat oven to 425°. In a 13x9 baking dish, coat with a non-stick spray and then butter the dish. In a separate bowl, combine flour, salt and pepper. Pour ½ cup of buttermilk into another bowl. Wash chicken pieces and removing excess skin. Dip chicken into the buttermilk then roll the pieces in the flour mixture. Place chicken in pan, breast side down. Bake uncovered for 30 minutes. Turn chicken breast side up. Mix remaining ¼ cup of buttermilk and soup and pour over the chicken and bake an additional 15 minutes reducing temperature to 400°. Use an internal thermometer and remove from oven when temperature reaches 175°.

Bear on the Square

Bear on the Square is an annual festival hosted by the Dahlonega Merchants Association. The history of the festival begins back in the spring of 1996 when a baby bear arrived on the public square and started trying to break into businesses. I was an eye witness to the event. My son, Evan Bafile, was at work with me. When we heard excitement break out on the square, we walked up the street to see that the cub had climbed up into a tall sycamore tree in front of Brad Walker's pottery shop, and was hanging onto a branch for dear life. As more people heard about it, a crowd gathered to see the excitement. At the time, we thought that the mother bear was still close by, so we kept an eye out for her. The DNR (Department of Natural Resources) sent out an officer who tranquilized the cub so that it would let go of the branch and fall out of the tree. A group of about 15 people held what looked like an Army blanket stretched out under the cub's branch to catch it when it fell. The cub slowly became drowsy, and the crowd gasped, and held its breath while it fell from the tree. It landed safely in the blanket, and the crowd went wild, laughing and crying and cheering. We found out later that his mother and brother had been captured by the DNR earlier in the day, and the cub was reunited with his family and returned to the wild.

Although this event was the catalyst for Dahlonega's festival, there was another bear incident on the square a century earlier. The original "bear on the square" happened in 1892 when a traveling show with trainers came to town. They charged an admission fee to show off their bears to a group of men outside of the Dahlonega courthouse. The trainers kept a close reign on the bears and drew a crowd to entertain. There are no women present in the photo below, which perhaps meant that it was not considered ladylike or proper for a woman to attend such a spectacle.

Dahlonega 1892. Bear Show. Three Frenchmen brought two bears to town.

Vanishing Georgia, Georgia Archives, University System of Georgia

Today, the bear on the square festival is a collection of the Southern Appalachian culture including bluegrass music, cultural art, and vendors from the area celebrating the monumental event that occurred years ago.

Smith House Baked Chicken

Mixture of chicken breast, thighs, and legs
1 teaspoon butter or margarine
¼ cup lemon juice
1 teaspoon paprika
1 teaspoon salt
½ teaspoon pepper
Optional: ¼ teaspoon granulated garlic

Preheat oven to 425. In a 13x9 baking dish, spray with a non-stick coating and butter dish. Wash chicken pieces and remove skin. Place chicken in the baking dish with the breast of the chicken down. In a separate bowl, mix lemon juice, salt, pepper, and garlic. Pour mixture over chicken pieces. Cover with aluminum foil. Bake in oven for 20 minutes then turn pieces of chicken over. Then bake for another 15 minutes without foil or until the internal temperature reads 175°.

Party Chicken Salad

4 chicken breast cooked (can use Smith House Baked Chicken recipe)
1 cup mayonnaise
½ cup sour cream
1 teaspoon lemon juice
½ teaspoon salt
¼ teaspoon pepper
1 cup chopped celery
1 granny smith apple
1-6ounce can of crushed pineapple, drained
1 cup grapes sliced in half
¼ cup of chopped walnuts

Shred cook chicken in a bowl. In a separate bowl, add mayonnaise, sour cream lemon juice, salt and pepper and stir to mix. Peel apple and cut into small cubes. Add apples, grapes, celery, and pineapple to the chicken. Pour mayonnaise mix and stir thoroughly. Fold in walnuts. Can be put into a mold and refrigerate overnight. Serve with crackers.

Smith House Roast Beef

3 pounds beef eye of round roast
½ teaspoon kosher salt
½ teaspoon garlic powder
¼ teaspoon pepper
3 carrots, cut into 3-inch parts
1 onion, quartered
3 diced potatoes
3 cloves of garlic

Remove roast from fridge 1-2 hours before cooking. Preheat oven to 375°. If roast is untied, tie at 3-inch intervals with cotton twine. Place roast in a pan, and season with salt, garlic powder, and pepper. Place carrots, garlic, potatoes and onion in bottom of pan. Tent the pan with aluminum foil and cook for 1 hour (20 minutes per pound). Reserve the juice from the pan. Let the roast rest for 20 minutes before slicing. Drizzle juice over pieces of beef before serving.

The Turkey Run

The wheel of the land lottery spun its last land lot in 1833, after seven months of granting lucky participants their tracks of land in the North Georgia Mountains. The ticket holder claimed their prize, some receiving up to 160 acres of the land district; others receiving some of the gold district's 40 acres lots. Not only did the prize winners move, but their whole family, some including field hands, moved as well. Supplies, especially food, soon started running out, and trips to nearby towns were usually a day's journey. The need for merchants became apparent to purchase items from potatoes and flour to picks and shovels. Mining companies purchased land from the ticket holders and had workers who needed food and supplies, and storehouses were quickly built to sell common living items and equipment. Dahlonega store prices during the 1830s were the following:

corn	75¢ to 87¢ / bushel
eggs	12¢ to 18¢ / dozen
flour	10¢ /pound
butter	18¢ to 20¢ / pound
potatoes	50¢ to 75¢ / bushel

Fresh meat was scarce and in high demand. The native Cherokees who escaped the exodus provided meat for the nearby citizens. The hunters would load their morning kills, which usually consisted of deer and wild turkey, on carts and ride through the town, selling their goods to locals and merchants. Occasionally, they surprised the townspeople with local honey from their bee hives. The Indians worked on a bartering system with the merchants for supplies they needed.

Evan's Wings-n-Things

10 chicken wings
Vegetable oil for deep fryer
Hot sauce
Lemon Juice
Melted butter
Pepper
Salt
Season Salt
Garlic

Wash chicken wings and fry in a deep fryer for 7-9 minutes. Meanwhile in a large bowl, mix remaining ingredients and mix. When the wings cooked, place in the bowl and toss. Cut celery and carrot sticks serve on a party tray with ranch dressing.

The Indians could supply only so much meat for the vast number of new citizens flooding the area, and another source was soon needed. Farmers from as far as Tennessee and Kentucky drove their livestock to North Georgia to sell. On the outskirts of town, pens were built to give these new pioneers the ability to buy from these traveling farmers. Livestock were usually brought from other states, and the sellers would showcase their animals in the pens to sell. The most challenging animals for the herders were turkeys. Townspeople were amused when the herders brought the turkeys to the area because the animals were hard to control. The workers would hurry to bring the turkeys to their locations to sell; if not done during daylight, the bird would fly up into the trees to roost upon evening time. If this was the case, herders had to be gentle and patiently wait until morning to gather the turkeys after they left the trees. If they were too harsh, the herders would make the birds would fly away.

I'll Fly Away

Some glad morning when this life is o'er,
I'll fly away;
To a home on God's celestial shore,
I'll fly away (I'll fly away)

Chorus
I'll fly away, Oh Glory
I'll fly away; (in the morning)
When I die, Hallelujah, by and by,
I'll fly away (I'll fly away).

When the shadows of this life have gone,
I'll fly away;
Like a bird from prison bars has flown,
I'll fly away (I'll fly away)
(Chorus)

Just a few more weary days and then,
I'll fly away;
To a land where joy shall never end,
I'll fly away (I'll fly away)
(Chorus)

Smith House Thanksgiving Turkey

1 turkey, approximately 15-25 pounds, thawed
2 cups of Chicken broth
1 cup unsalted butter, melted
1 teaspoon salt
1 teaspoon pepper
1 teaspoon granulated garlic (optional)

Remove turkey from fridge and let sit at room temperature for 30 minutes. Preheat oven to 450°. Remove the bag of giblets from the cavity of the bird. Set the turkey on a roasting rack breast side up. Rub the turkey with the ½ cup of butter then with the salt, pepper, and garlic. If preferred can add stuffing or vegetables to cavity of the bird. Pour the chicken broth over the turkey and the juices will gather at the bottom of the pan. Plan to baste the turkey every 45 minutes while cooking in oven. Cook in the oven for the first 45 minutes.

Cooking time: 13 minutes for every pound of turkey.
After the first 45 minutes, remove turkey and baste with juices that gathered at bottom of cooking pan. Do this for every 45 minutes and if the turkey looks like the skin is burning, cover with aluminum foil. In the last 45 minutes, baste with juices and with the ½ cup of butter. Check the temperature of the meat and if the thermometer reads 165°, move from oven and let rest for 30 minutes before serving.
Serve with Dressing and Smith House Cranberry Relish

Smith House Baked Ham

1 (12 pound) bone-in ham un-cooked
1 cup packed brown sugar
½ cup whole cloves
4 cups water
Optional: 1 teaspoon brown or Dijon mustard and ½ cup maple syrup
Optional: 1 can of pineapple slices, drained and 1 (10 ounce) jar maraschino cherries drained

Preheat oven to 350°. Place ham in a foil lined shallow roasting pan, and press whole cloves into the ham. Pack the top with a layer of brown sugar. Pour enough water into the bottom of the roasting pan to come to a 1-inch depth. Cover the pan tightly with aluminum foil. Bake for 4½ to 5 hours. If using the optional ingredients, take the ham out after 4 hours and boil mustard and maple syrup and pour over ham. If preferred, add pineapple with cherries over top of ham (can use toothpicks to keep in place). Put back in oven for remainder of time. The internal temperature should be 160°. Let the meat rest for 20 minutes before carving into desired slices.

Court's in Session

Replica of a c.1830 building
Vanishing Georgia, Georgia Archives,
University System of Georgia

Dahlonega was chosen as the location of the county seat. A log house was built in the middle of the town; it was a small building with dimensions of 18 x 32 feet, constructed of split logs and pine poles. The narrow door was 3 feet wide, and the height was short so that an average-sized man had to stoop to enter.

The first session of court convened on August 22, 1833, where His Honor, Judge John W. Cooper took his seat and gavel and called the court to order. Mostly present were bearded miners, citizens of Auraria, and in the back of the room, curious Cherokee Indians. The first bill of the court involved the murder of Robert Ligon, the postmaster of Auraria. Jessie N. Brown was convicted of the crime and sentenced. The second bill concerned the citizens of Auraria. The town hosted many brawling miners over mining spots or drunken fights. Several men were being convicted of the gambling crimes of "chuck a luck" for operating illegal gambling tables. Lastly, the third order of business concerned plans to build a bigger courthouse and a new jail as soon as possible.

The idea of a new and bigger courthouse for the town had a difficult beginning. The first transaction given to John Humphries promised completion in eight months with an advance payment of $2500 for supplies. Humphries, being a dishonest person, took the money and headed out of town. The second contract proved a success under Ephraim Clayton. A two-story brick building was completed in 1836. The payment made to Clayton was in gold bouillons, and the bricks were molded at the Brickyard Hill from clay of the heavy, rich soil bearing gold of the North Georgia Mountains. On a bright and sunny day, flecks of gold would shine through the bricks. The gold-lined streets of Dahlonega were the effect of the heavy rains that washed the gold from the brick foundation of the courthouse.

What is "Chuck-a-luck?" The game is played with three standard dice and a layout numbered from 1-6 on each side, upon which the players placed their bets. The banker rolls the dice by turning over the hourglass-shaped wire cage or a cone-shaped chute (made of leather or metal and called a horn) in which they are contained. The playoffs are usually 1 to 1 on singles, 2 to 1 on pairs, and 3 to 1 on triples appearing on the dice. Early on, this game was played with gamblers who had little money. The dice was thrown or "chucked" across the board and the numbers revealed the winner. Later the wire cage was introduced.

Country Fried Steak

- 3 pounds of cube steak
- 3 tablespoons vegetable oil
- ¼ cup all-purpose flour
- ¼ cup seasoned bread crumbs
- 1 egg
- 2 teaspoons water
- ½ teaspoon salt
- ½ teaspoon pepper

In a separate bowl, mix flour, salt, pepper, and bread crumbs. In another bowl, beat egg and water. Take the cube steaks and coat flour mixture, then dip into egg mixture and coat again with the flour mixture. In a large skillet, cook steaks in oil over medium heat for 2 minutes on each side, or until meat reaches desired doneness. Remove and keep warm.

Country Gravy

- 2 tablespoons all-purpose flour
- 1 ¼ cups milk
- ¼ teaspoon salt
- ¼ teaspoon pepper

Stir flour, salt and pepper into pan drippings until blended, loosening browned bits. Gradually stir in milk. Bring to a boil over medium heat. Whisk for 2 minutes or until thickened. Pour gravy over steaks.

Sweet and Sour Meatballs

- 1 pound ground beef
- 1 egg
- ¼ cup dry bread crumbs
- 2 tablespoons vegetable oil
- 1 diced onion

Sweet and sour sauce

- 1 cup brown sugar
- 3 tablespoons all-purpose flour
- 1 ½ cups water
- ¼ cup white vinegar
- 3 tablespoons soy sauce

In a bowl, combine beef, egg, bread crumbs, and onion and mix thoroughly. Shape into small round balls. In a fry pan, turn stove on medium heat with oil and when oil is hot, add the meatballs. Take a fork and when browned move the balls around until browned.

In a saucepan, combine brown sugar, flour, water, vinegar and soy sauce and bring to a boil. Stir mixture so it doesn't burn for 30 minutes. Remove from heat and add drained meatballs.

Barbecue Pork

- 3 pounds boneless pork shoulder roast
- 1 (14 ounce) can beef broth

Sauce

- ¼ cup ketchup
- 2 tablespoons brown sugar
- 1 tablespoon cider vinegar
- 1 teaspoon garlic powder
- ¼ teaspoon mustard powder
- ¼ teaspoon salt
- 2 tablespoons Worcestershire sauce

Pour can of beef broth into slow cooker, and add roast. Cook on high heat for 4 hours or until meat shreds easily. To make sauce, in a sauce pan add ingredients under sauce recipe and bring to a slow boil. Remove from heat and stirring constantly. Remove the meat, and shred with two forks. Preheat oven to 350°. Transfer the shredded pork to a Dutch oven or iron skillet, and stir in barbeque sauce. Bake at 350 degree for 30 minutes.

Destruction

Side of the 1836 Court House - picture c.1936
Vanishing Georgia, Georgia Archives, University System of Georgia

The fate of the 1836 Dahlonega Courthouse hung in the balance with local merchants and historians wanting the purpose of the land for different reasons. A new courthouse was built in 1965 east of the public square. The 1836 courthouse was converted into the Dahlonega Gold Museum.

Merchants on the square were looking at the location of the old 1836 courthouse for additional parking, as visitor parking in town was limited. However, other locals did not want to see this history marker to be destroyed and never remembered. History enthusiasts wanted the old courthouse to be preserved as a museum displaying artifacts of the gold rush days. The Georgia Historical Commission supervised the project of renovating the building into what is known today as the Dahlonega Gold Museum. When the needed documents were moved to the new location, there were many other documents the new building could not store. The officials looked at the old handwritten titles, property deeds, family pictures, and promissory notes as "rubbish." Ms. Madeline Anthony, a local historian, confronted the issue with fire in her bones and took it upon herself to save the documents from the landfills. The "Madeline Anthony Files" consist of the documents and pictures she saved from destruction. Sallie Sorohan compiled the files together for the local library. This preserved history was the main source used for research while producing the Smith House DVD and also contributed to this cookbook.

1836 Court House - picture c.1880
Vanishing Georgia, Georgia Archives, University System of Georgia

Ms. Anthony proudly opened the doors of the Dahlonega Gold Museum on June 1, 1967. People came from all over to visit the museum and Dahlonega. She would share her knowledge and the historical aspects that built the town. Ms. Anthony marked visitors' states on a map, and her goal was for every state to be represented at the gold museum. With Alaska being a missing part, she voiced her concern to the local sheriff. To his surprise, shortly after their conversation, a visiting car to Dahlonega displayed the tag of Alaska. The car was pulled over and would not be released until they visited the Gold Museum.

Present Day Dahlonega Gold Museum

Fried Shrimp

1½ pounds raw shrimp, peeled and deveined (fresh or frozen)
2 eggs beaten
1 teaspoon salt
½ cup self-rising flour
½ cup dry bread crumbs
½ teaspoon paprika
½ teaspoon pepper
¼ teaspoon garlic salt
Vegetable oil for frying

Thaw shrimp if frozen. Combine egg and salt. Combine flour, bread crumbs and paprika. Dip each shrimp in egg, then roll in crumb mixture. Fry in a basket in a deep fryer with vegetable oil for 350° for 2 to 3 minutes, or until golden brown. Drain and serve with chili or tartar sauce.

Boiled Shrimp

2 pounds raw shrimp, fresh or frozen
5 cups of water
2 tablespoons salt
One bag crab boil
½ can of beer

Thaw shrimp if frozen. Peel and devein shrimp. Rinse shrimp thoroughly and drain. Add salt to water and bring to a boil with the crab boil and beer. Add shrimp and reduce heat. Cover and simmer 3 to 4 minutes, or until the largest shrimp is opaque in the center. (Jumbo shrimp will require more cooking time). Drain shrimp and rinse thoroughly for 1 to 2 minutes under cold water. Serve.

Tarter Sauce

1 20-ounce jar of mayonnaise
½ onion, thinly sliced and grated
2 tablespoons lemon juice
½ cup sweet and dill relish
1 tablespoon grated garlic

Thinly cut onions and grate. In a bowl, mix mayonnaise, onion, lemon juice, sweet and dill relish, and garlic. Mix well with onions and adjust ingredients to taste.

Cocktail Sauce

1 8-ounce can of chili sauce
1 8-ounce can tomato sauce
2 tablespoons worcestershire sauce
4 ounces of horseradish sauce (add more if you like your sauce spicy)

Mix all ingredients into a bowl and stir thoroughly.

Court's in Session
LIFE magazine
September 21, 1942, issue

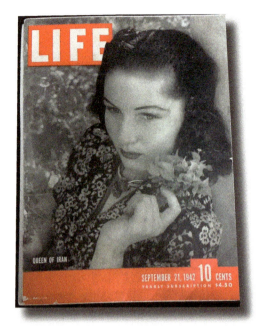

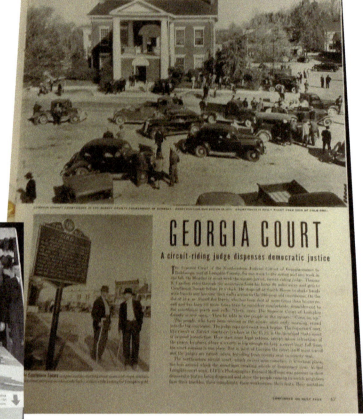

The caption under the picture on the bottom of the next page (*LIFE* magazine page 76) reads, "Meals during court week are always special. Almost every county seat has one hostelry where the judges, the important lawyers and the well-to-do-clients eat. In Dahlonega it is the Smith House where the proprietor himself presides at the table head. Passing him a plate is Judge Candler. At right sits Mrs. Townsend. The light lunch includes roast beef, pork, chicken, sweet potatoes, beans, greens, corn bread, tomatoes, preserves. Ben Smith, who is in politics, prides himself on feeding his guests well any time, but during court week he outdoes himself."

Mr. Smith, owner of the Smith House, serving the judges a family style dinner at his residence.

Smith House

Vegetables

Battlebranch Goldmine

Battlebranch Goldmine certainly saw its share of fighting and disagreements during the 1800s. The mine, located in present day Auraria, was given the awarded name Nuckollsville. Since disputes between miners were very common, the name either came from the bare-knuckle fighting of the miners settling their disputes, or after Nathaniel Nuckolls who built a hotel there in 1832. Traders from Tennessee visited the mining camps to sell food items and, watching the miners extract gold nuggets out of their pans, soon decided that they themselves were better off panning gold than selling goods.

Georgian miners were not going to give up their gold without a fight.

The 1832 Land Lottery began in the fall of that year, and people poured into the region in great numbers. In one year, the town population grew quickly to 10,000 and included 100 homes, 18 stores, a dozen law offices, and five taverns. Six months prior, there were scarcely any white people in the territory, except for soldiers guarding the mines and several surveying parties who were divided off the land lots as rapidly as possible. By November of the same year, Nuckollsville had a substantial population and received its official name of Auraria at the suggestion of John C. Calhoun, Vice-President of the United States from 1825-1832. Calhoun resided in the area because of his mining interests.

In April of 1833, an election was held for the purpose of determining which town, either Auraria or Dahlonega, would be the county seat. Auraria was the older and larger of the two choices, and the town had been settled for ten months. Dahlonega could put forth no such claim to age, population, or wealth, but its location was an advantage. At first, Auraria seemed more ideal than Dahlonega, but the "lot" on which the principal part of Auraria was located had been fraudulently drawn in the land lottery, making the title defective. Since there was little time to straighten out the land issue, Dahlonega was chosen to be the county seat, set in the county's center so that the miners would have a central location from all areas of the gold region.

The Battlebranch Gold Mine showed a profit for many years and continued producing gold well into the 1900s, and in 1935 the mine had 661.28 ounces of gold recorded. However, gold production eventually started to diminish, and so did the town of Auraria.

Auraria picture of the famous two-headed cow.
Vanishing Georgia, Georgia Archives, University System of Georgia

Smith House Creamed Corn

8 ears corn, husked
1 tablespoon sugar
1 tablespoon all-purpose flour
½ teaspoon salt
¼ tablespoon black pepper
½ cup whole milk
1 tablespoon butter

Husk the corn, removing all hair from the corn. Cut the tips off of the cob and wash. Cut the kernels from cob with a small paring knife. Take a butter knife and scrape off the natural juice of the corn. In a saucepan on medium-heat, whisk together milk and flour then add sugar, corn juice, salt and pepper. Add corn and butter to pan and bring to a light boil then turn heat down to medium low, stirring until it becomes creamy, about 15 minutes.

Skillet Corn

¼ cup of butter
2½ cup corn (cut off the cob if available)
½ cup half and half cream
1 teaspoon cornstarch
1 teaspoon sugar
½ teaspoon salt (or to taste)
¼ teaspoon pepper

In a large skillet, melt butter over medium heat. Add corn, cream, cornstarch, sugar, salt and pepper and bring to a boil stirring constantly. Reduce heat and cook for 15 minutes.

A Three-Day Ration

During the 1830s, "Gold Fever" had struck just about everyone in the region. News of Ben Park's gold find in the North Georgia Mountains quickly spread, and the excitement extended to many people in far-off regions who came to the area to "strike it rich." They came on foot, horseback, and wagons. Farmers, lawyers, doctors, preachers, women, and children came from all over the country with their picks, shovels, and pans in hand to find their riches. There were men panning out of branches and making holes in the hillsides. The miner's philosophy was "if I found it, then it is mine."

Disregarding the land dealings between the United States and Cherokee Nation, many disputes between the Cherokee Indians and white miners occurred. Miners would sneak onto Indian land and mine their gold, so the Cherokees regarded miners as "intruders." The Georgia Assembly enacted legislation declaring that any persons digging for gold, unless authorized, were to be arrested and sentenced in the state penitentiary for four years. The law found little respect from the miners, therefore Georgia Troops were sent into the region to mandate control. Three hundred troops came to the gold region in September 1830 and were stationed between the Chestatee and Etowah Rivers to make their arrests.

The Cherokee Indians became less tolerant of the situation and, looking for ways for the miners to leave, brought their complaints to the U.S. government. Not only did the miners cause problems, but members of the Pony Club did even more damage to the Indians' lifestyle. This ruthless group of white men would band together and ride nightly across the area to cause death and destruction along their way. Families were taken from their homes, houses burned, and livestock stolen or killed. To control the chaos happening in the North Georgia Mountains, the government sent Army regulars to establish order with the Pony Club and also illegal mining that was taking place. However, the miners coming to the area illegally were willing to take the risk of jail time.

The intruders crossed over the Chestatee River and into Cherokee territory every night and filled large sacks with gravel, known as placer deposits. After their bags were filled, they crossed back before daybreak so they would not get caught on Indian land. The federal troops assigned to the area found it hard to patrol the vast amount of land with only three hundred men. Some of the Indians helped the troops capture these trespassers. However, the Indians found themselves in violation of their rights by arresting the white men, even though they were working under the law of the United States. The soldiers would pack a three-day ration of food and supplies so they would be able to patrol for longer time periods. A typical U.S. Army ration decreed by the Continental Congress would include: meat or salt fish, bread or hard tack (cracker or biscuit made from flour, water, and sometimes salt), and vegetables. Before the 1800s, a soldier was sent with 2-4 ounces of rum depending upon their trip duration. However, after the 1800s the rum was replaced with a ration of sugar and coffee.

The miners, knowing the patrols were coming more frequently, grouped together to signal to each other when they heard the troops coming. The groups would place watchmen around the troops to keep track of their whereabouts. Soldiers would close in on the miners, but the watchman would signal the alarm and miners would scatter in all directions. Miners were captured, but others outran the soldiers and hid in the vast forest. They waited in hiding and when the coast was clear, gathered back to see who was left. They headed back to the rivers to mine again and waited on the next signal.

Smith House Cabbage Casserole

- 1 large cabbage head
- 1 teaspoon of salt
- 1 can cream of mushroom or chicken soup
- ½ cup crisp bacon, crumbled
- 1 cup shredded carrots
- Cheddar cheese, to top casserole

Pre-heat oven to 350°. Wash and slice cabbage in quarters and tear apart the leaves and discarding the core. In a large pot, bring 4 cups of water, cabbage, carrots, and salt. Steam until tender, then drain. Meanwhile, cook bacon until brown and set aside. Mix soup with cabbage together. In a casserole dish, add cabbage then top with crumbled bacon and top with grated cheese. Bake for 20-30 minutes.

Smith House Squash Casserole

- 4 cups sliced yellow squash
- ½ cup chopped onions
- 1 can cream of chicken soup
- 1 teaspoon salt
- ½ cup sour cream
- 1 cup grated cheese
- ¼ cup of butter, melted
- 1 cup toasted bread or crumbled Ritz® crackers

Pre-heat oven to 350°. In a large sauce pan, cover squash and onions with water and add salt. Cook until tender about 5 minutes, and then drain well. Mix squash and onions with soup and sour cream, and pour half of the mixture in a casserole dish. In a separate bowl, mix melted butter with crackers. Pour ½ squash mixture into a casserole dish and layer half the buttered crackers and repeat layer and pour ½ stick melted butter over top of casserole. Sprinkle with bread crumbs and bake at 350° for 30-40 minutes or until bread crumbs are browned.

A Twist of Fate

1830 Cherokee Lands

The Cherokee lands were distributed to the people of the state by means of a land lottery system. On October 22, 1833 the state of Georgia started spinning the twin drums in Milledgeville to reveal the fortunate winners. Two drums were used: one for the ticket holder name and the other for the land lot number. Both drums spun simultaneously, and one ticket was drawn from each. Between 1805 and 1827 five lotteries occurred to parcel out Indian land. The lottery of 1832, the sixth and final one, expelled the Indians from the land. The old Cherokee lands were divided up into 35,000 lots, with 133,000 names registered to draw. Blank papers were placed into the barrels and three out of four people walked away empty handed. The winner made an oath that he or she was qualified and paid an $18 grant fee.

To be eligible and qualify for a ticket for a 160-acre lot, one could be a white male over the age of 16; a widow or a family of an orphan; heads of families; veterans and orphans of veterans; a citizen of Georgia for four or more years. Families with more than one orphan had more chances to obtain a ticket. Barred from the ticket process were illegal miners, members of the Pony Club, people who had received land in previous lotteries, and the Cherokee Indians. Freed Blacks and slaves were brought in to help the land owners build the properties and mine for gold. Ten counties were made out of this one area.

Lumpkin County was formed by the Act of Georgia Legislature on December 3, 1832. Dahlonega was made the county seat during April of 1833. It had not been officially named yet, but the village was referred to both as Talonega (Cherokee for yellow or gold color) and Licklog. Public concern was shared in the way the land was distributed. Many believed that it was a terrible waste of the state's wealth, and some shared the feelings that the state should operate the mines instead of individual owners. The influx of money into the system would lower taxes, build new and upgrade older roads, make rivers more navigable, and generate public education. The lottery system was chosen to avoid land disputes, but many believed it would only heighten speculations of land titles. Fraud occurred from rapid buying and selling of land after the lotteries, with both the state and individual land owners.

10 Counties created from the original Cherokee County	
Forsyth	Lumpkin
Union	Cobb
Cherokee	Gilmer
Cass(Bartow)	Murray
Floyd	Paulding

Mining companies were eager to buy gold lots from the lucky recipients. The Pigeon Roost lot was one of the richest mining lots in Dahlonega, and the Jefferson Mining Company waited eagerly for the announcement of the winner. The lucky man was a poor farmer who worked on a nearby plantation. The company offered the farmer $10,000 for the property, and he proudly accepted the lump sum of money. A second account revolved around Land Lot No. 1052 on Yahoola Creek. Another farmer, Alford Allison, won the ticket and was approached by a man named Mosley, who wanted the lot because it was known to have a considerable amount of gold. The farmer hesitated at the idea and then offered a wholesome amount that almost sent Mosley into bankruptcy. After his acquisition, Mosley purchased equipment for his new mine. He could not bring in enough gold to pay off his endeavors and had to sell the mine. Allison, the original ticket holder, purchased the mine back for a fraction of the cost of the original price. Soon after the change of ownership, a rich vein was found on the property, and great wealth came to the first lottery ticket holder, Mr. Allison.

Smith House Black-eyed Peas

1 pound dried black-eyed peas
½ teaspoon salt
4 cups water or beef broth
¼ teaspoons black pepper
1 large onion, chopped
½ pound pork or lean ham, cut into pieces

Soak peas in lightly salted water overnight. Drain peas and place in a crock pot with water, pepper, chopped onion, and meat. Cook on high heat for 2 hours, then on low for 6-7 hours. Serve with cornbread!

Baked Beans

2 cups dry navy beans
1 teaspoon salt
1½ quarts cold water
1 teaspoon dry mustard
1 teaspoon salt
½ cup molasses
½ cup brown sugar
1 medium onion, finely chopped
¼ pound of pork or bacon

Rinse beans and soak beans overnight in cold water. Pour water and beans into a sauce pan and bring to a full boil, then lower heat and simmer for 10 minutes. Cover and remove from heat, add salt and let stand for one hour. Drain beans and reserve bean water. In a sauce pan, combine ¾ cup of bean liquid with sugar, salt, mustard, and molasses and bring to a boil. Cut pork into pieces. In a 2-quart casserole dish, alternate layers of beans, onion, pork, and sugar mixture. Repeat layers. Cover with aluminum foil and bake at 325° for 3 hours. Remove foil one hour before done and add more liquid if needed.

The Safety Man

A resurgence of gold mining took place in Dahlonega after miners returned from California in 1850 with new ways of extracting gold from the earth, instead of panning the streams. Hydraulic mining, commonly used in California, involved the construction of canals to transport water from high mountain streams to the mines. The water, pulled down by gravity, was funneled into a giant hose (called a monitor), and the elevation of the canals provided enough force to wash tons of dirt from the mountains. The mountains took a beating from this method of mining, and landscapes washed away to reveal the rich quartz rocks.

Alongside this form of mining was rock blasting. Miners dug tunnels and shafts, and the rocks were blasted with either dynamite or gun powder. Shafts presented more dangerous outcomes for the miners. A safety man was the one who had the most critical job. Not an avid miner himself, but perhaps not smart enough to value his life, the safety man's fate solely relied on the dynamite firing at the appropriate time. He was lowered down the shaft in a basket, and a light-weight person was commonly used for the ease of lowering and bringing the basket back up to the surface. The safety man dug a hole in the shaft and inserted gunpowder and fuses, working at a steady pace in line with the other miners. His life depended upon accuracy. The men signaled to each other when they finished placing the dynamite to light the fuse, and then they quickly waved for the others to pull them out of the shaft. One slip of the hand would be death to the one in the basket. Men are yelling "hurry, hurry," while the sound of pulleys creaked and brought the man to the surface. When they reached the surface, everyone ran for cover and then anxiously awaited the big boom. Unfortunately, some miners were not as lucky and were caught in the explosion.

A Hunting Party c.1900
Vanishing Georgia, Georgia Archives, University System of Georgia

Coal was used to produce electricity during the early mining process and was soon replaced by using the water from the Chestatee River to turn turbine wheels that supplied power. The mines operated 24 hours, with two shifts a day. Most miners suffered from lung problems from the dust created by the dynamite. The safety man was the highest paid of the miners, collecting wages of $2.50 daily. The other miners received their pay either on a weekly or monthly draw.

Smith House Green Beans

1 pound fresh green beans
6 cups water
1 ham hock or 1 pound of bacon
1 teaspoon salt
1 teaspoon black pepper
Optional: 6 red or new potatoes cut into quarters

Wash beans thoroughly, pat to dry. String the beans and snap into bite size pieces. In a large pot, combine water and ham hock and to a boil. Add the beans and season with salt and pepper. Bring to a boil, and then reduce heat to medium-low for the first 30 minutes then reduce heat to a simmer covered for about 2 hours. If adding potatoes, add to cooking pot after 1 hour of cooking beans.

Green Bean Casserole

4 cups cooked green beans or 2 cans green beans, drained
1 can cream of mushroom soup
½ cup milk
1 can French's Fried Onion

In a greased baking dish, layer green beans and top with ½ can of onion rings. Combine soup and milk; pour mixture over green beans. Repeat layers and bake at 350° until bubbling. Place the final layer with onion rings on top. Bake until the onion rings are toasted, about 20-30 minutes.

They Called Her Amazon

In the early 1800s, the Cherokees became frustrated with the unwanted miners that came upon their land to mine their streams and steal their gold. The Indians used gold for trading in their culture. Confrontations between them were usual occurrences, the natives and eagerly wanted the U.S. government to step up and provide a peaceful solution to the problem. One certain confrontation occurred at a stream in Dahlonega. An Indian woman staked claims to the area around the stream and was known by the miners as being a wild woman. They described her as being almost nude, wearing war paint, and that she had a powerful frame for a woman. Her ploy was to wait on the miners to set up panning at the stream and then violently jump out at them from a shaft. She thrashed at the white man that stole her gold. Her name became Amazon, and miners named the area the Amazon branch.

After the establishment of the town, miners who found their efforts of gold digging to be unsuccessful turned to mercantilism. One of these miners-turned-merchants was Harrison Riley. Riley came to Dahlonega in 1833 upon hearing the rumors of the great wealth in the Georgia Mountains, but decided to leave the dirty work for others. Riley was one of the first settlers in Dahlonega and opened up several operations for the miners. He opened the first tavern, store, and hotel. Riley's tavern and gambling saloon was located on the public square, where the Smith House Chestatee Village sits today, and by 1838 he established his riches. The tavern had an upstairs bridge that crossed over the road to his hotel, The Riley Hotel (later The Eagle Hotel), which is located across from the present-day Dahlonega Gold Museum.

Vanishing Georgia, Georgia Archives, University System of Georgia

Reports of many shoot-outs and scuffles of spirited men occurred in the 1840-50s. Miners traveled to town frequently to visit the tavern and spent their gold on drinks and gambling. The saloon housed gambling, dancing, drinking, and womenfolk waiting on the miners to come to town. Gambling favorites of the miners include chuck-a-luck, dice, cards, pushpin, and horse racing, all of which the saloon was eager to offer day and night. This furthered the violence in the area because of claims of cheating and disagreements between drunken participants. The bar owner would hire men to escort such people to the town's Tanyard (Amazon) branch at the end of Water Street. They referred to the spot as the "Sprawls Hotel." The branch, also known as the Amazon River, was a large brook that brought healing properties to their victims. The workers escorted the drunks to the branch and threw them in for immediate relief of their madness. If this did not work, the intoxicated man was allowed to "ooze himself" until he was sober enough to check out on his own. Luckily, there were no reports of life lost during these sobering sessions.

Riley is noted to be one of the wealthiest men in the state upon his death in 1874. The Tanyard branch location was just below the Smith House, where the University of North Georgia has their parking deck and athletic center. The Smith House kept the branch's memory alive by naming the public dining room the Tanyard Room, symbolizing the mining history in Dahlonega.

Creamy Mashed Potatoes

6 medium russet potatoes, peeled and cubed
½ cup warm milk
1 cup sour cream
¼ cup butter or margarine
1 teaspoon salt
1 teaspoon pepper

Place potatoes in a saucepan with salted water. Bring to a boil and cook for 18-20 minutes, or until very tender. Drain, and in a mixing bowl add potatoes, milk, sour cream, butter, salt, and pepper. Blend until completely smooth.

Thanksgiving Rice Dish

4 cups of cooked rice
½ stick butter
1 rib of celery, finely chopped
1 (4 ounce) jar pimentos, drained
1 green bell pepper, finely chopped
2 tablespoons lemon juice
1 teaspoon salt

Cook rice according to directions (can use long grain rice). In a sauce pan, add butter, celery, pimentos, peppers, lemon juice, and salt and cook until tender. Add rice to sauce pan and stir. Enjoy!

Fred Welch Sr., Operator and Owner of the Smith House from 1946-1980

Mr. Bill Fry purchased the Smith House in 1946 and needed somebody to run the dining room and kitchen for him. In an interview with *The Dahlonega Nugget* printed on May 3, 1990, Fred Welch told the story of when Mr. Fry wanted both him and his wife Thelma to operate the dining room.

"Bill Littlefield recommended me, Fred told, and when Mr. Fry asked me about the business proposition, I told him I'd have to study about it. He told me he would make me a good deal, and he did. The first day, Thelma and I took over; we were responsible for serving the Lions' Club banquet. We were lucky about getting good cooks. Fred Riley was already the head cook under the former owners, the Smiths, and could cook exceptionally well. He was especially good at seasoning vegetables to perfection. Mrs. Fry was a lot of help to us, too. She taught Thelma to make the rolls that became such an important item on the Smith House menu. Up until that time, only biscuits had been served.

My daddy, Arthur "Pat" Welch, was a jack of all trades who could do most anything from building furniture to electrical wiring, plumbing, and wallpapering. At one time he ran the ice plant at the old Mountain Lodge. My mother, Laura Beck Welch, taught me to be a good cook. She was cooking for the Cavenders sisters at their restaurant next to Jake's grill. I started helping out there. Later, I started cooking for the restaurant/bus station Fred Jones operated on the public square of Dahlonega. After that I worked for Vernon Smith, son of Henry and Bessie Smith, former owners of the Smith House, when he was running a sandwich shop. There was no canteen on the college campus, and every hour when the bell rang, there would be a big rush of students coming in for drinks, hotdogs, hamburgers, and sandwiches. After I got off of work I would stop in at the College Inn (located presently at the Jean Moore building) for a hamburger because Thelma Ray was working there. Sometimes we would go bowling together at the center next door to where she worked. We soon married on June 19, 1942.

When Thelma and I took over the Smith House, she did a lot of the cooking, but it took all my time doing the buying and just keeping up with everything. Farmers would bring their produce to sell us, but I also hauled a lot from the Farmer's Market in Atlanta, especially during the winter months. The kitchen and dining room were located on the main floor of the main building when we first went there, and we could only seat forty people. A few years later we finished the lower area and moved the eating facilities downstairs. We served three meals a day, seven days a week for nearly 25 years. Normal hours started at 7:00 a.m.-8:00 p.m., and if people came in later than that we would heat up some food and serve them.

We bought the Smith House from W.B. Fry in 1970. Our son, Freddy and his wife, Shirley came into the business with us a couple years before that, and they have been running it since Thelma and I retired in 1980. The business is a lot more complicated these days than it used to be when we first took over. Even after retirement I continued to work in the business. You might say that cooking is in my blood."

Smith House Macaroni and Cheese

1 box (8 ounces) macaroni noodles
3 cups milk
¼ cup of butter
3 tablespoons of all-purpose flour
Salt and pepper, to taste
2 cups cheddar cheese

Topping (optional)
2 cups of Italian bread crumbs or 1 sleeve of Ritz® crackers
1 cup parmesan cheese
2 tablespoons of butter

Preheat oven to 350°. Bring to a boil noodles in salted water. Cook until almost done, approximately 7 minutes, then drain. Place noodles in a casserole dish. In a sauce pan, cook on medium heat, melt butter and flour and make a roux, slowly add milk, salt and cheese and whisk until smooth or until cheese is melted. Pour mixture over noodles. Mix bread crumbs, butter and cheese together and top the casserole Bake at 300° for 30 minutes. Remove from oven. If the mixture looks soupy, cook for another 15 minutes.

Candied Sweet Potatoes
by Fred Welch Sr.

4 large sweet potatoes, peeled and cut into cubes
¼ cup butter or margarine
¼ cup maple syrup
¼ cup packed brown sugar
¼ teaspoon cinnamon
¼ teaspoon lemon juice

Cook potatoes in a pot with water and bring to a boil. Lower heat and cook until potatoes are tender. Drain potatoes and place in a casserole baking dish. In a small saucepan, combine remaining ingredients. Cook and stir until mixture boils. Pour over potatoes. Bake at 350° for 40 minutes.

Fred Welch, Jr., Operator of the Smith House from 1970 - Present

Smith House Candied Yams
by Freddy Welch

6 large sweet potatoes, peeled and quartered
2 ½ cups white sugar
½ cup lemon juice
1 cup water
2 fresh lemons, cut in halves

In a large sauce pan add potatoes, sugar, lemon juice, water and lemons; stir to dissolve sugar. Allow to stand for 15 minutes, and then cook over medium heat until potatoes are tender (approximately one hour).

Sweet Potato Casserole

Preheat oven to 350°. Grease a large casserole dish. In a bowl, mix 2 cups cooked and mashed sweet potatoes and the following ingredients in a mixer until smooth. Pour into greased baking dish.

1 teaspoon vanilla
2 eggs
1 cup milk
½ teaspoon nutmeg
1 cup sugar
½ teaspoon cinnamon
1 stick of melted butter

Topping

1 cup coconut
1 cup chopped pecans
1 cup brown sugar
1/3 cup flour
1/3 cup melted butter

Mix coconut, nuts, brown sugar, butter, and flour in a separate bowl. Pour mixture over the casserole and bake in oven for 25 minutes or until golden brown.

There's Millions in It

The 1836 Dahlonega Courthouse has heard many cases throughout its history, from mining and land disputes to theft and murders. The most noted historical event that happened there was on the second story of the building when the local assayer proclaimed to the miners leaving Dahlonega for California to not leave the local mines. The miners were frustrated over the quantity of gold they were panning in the creeks; the little amount was not worth risking their lives for.

When the gold rush in Georgia was believed to be over, many miners headed west to join the 1849 California Gold Rush. Dr. M.F. Stephenson, assayer at the Dahlonega Mint, was concerned for the economic problem this would cause the town. He stood on the courthouse steps, urging the miners to stay, pointing to the Findley Ridge. Dr. Stephenson proclaimed to over 200 men, "Why go to California? In that ridge lies more gold than man ever dreamt of. There's millions in it."

This excerpt was retold to Mark Twain by the miners who left for California from Georgia and may have inspired his character Mulberry Sellers. The character was famous for his lines "There's gold in them thar hills" and "there's millions in it" in the book The Gilded Ages.

"There's Millions in It!"

The Gilded Age and the Economy of Satire

Tracy Wuster

Beautiful credit! The foundation of modern society. Who shall say that this is not the golden age of mutual trust, of unlimited reliance upon human promises? That is a peculiar condition of society which enables a whole nation to instantly recognize point and meaning in the familiar newspaper anecdote, which puts into the mouth of a distinguished speculator in lands and mines this remark:—"I wasn't worth a cent two years ago, and now I owe two millions of dollars."

—Mark Twain and Charles Dudley Warner,
The Gilded Age

With the introduction of the character of Colonel Beriah Sellers, Mark Twain created a rollicking satire of small-town speculators caught up in a newly nationalized economy that few, if any, truly understood. The advent of beautiful credit, and its foundation in the railroads that were rapidly expanding throughout the nation, put Sellers at the center of an American drama that Twain, and his coauthor Charles Dudley Warner, portrayed as a farce of national proportions. Published in 1873, *The Gilded Age* marks an important development in Twain's career as a writer, and its topic—the current state of American life, or in the words of its subtitle "A Tale of To-Day"—represents Twain's first and only attempt at a sustained satire of contemporary American life. *The Gilded Age* has been largely elided in Twain scholarship as a failed production sitting between his early sketches and travel books and his turn to the subject of the river with "Old Times on the Mississippi" and *The Adventures of Tom Sawyer*. As a literary event and a literary curiosity, the book received substantial attention, and its promotion, reception, and transformations illuminate important facets of literary production in the era that it encapsulated, satirized, and ultimately named.

Smith House Broccoli and Rice Casserole

- 2 packages of frozen broccoli or two fresh bunches steamed
- 1 can cream of mushroom or chicken soup
- 1 cup cooked rice, cooled
- 1 onion, finely chopped
- ½ stick margarine or butter
- ¼ cup water
- ½ cup milk
- 1 cup of bread crumbs or one sleeve of Ritz® crackers
- 1 cup grated cheese

Heat oven to 350°. Bring to a boil salted water enough to cover broccoli and cook until tender. Drain broccoli and let cool. Chop broccoli into smaller pieces. Sauté onion in butter or margarine and mix broccoli, rice, water, milk, ½ cup of cheese, and onion. Place into a greased casserole dish. Top casserole with bread crumbs and remaining cheese. Bake in oven for 30 minutes.

Smith House Fried Okra

- 1 pound okra
- 2 cups of buttermilk
- 1 cups yellow cornmeal
- 1 cup self-rising flour
- ½ teaspoon salt
- ½ teaspoon pepper
- 6 cups oil, for frying

Wash okra and cut off ends of the stems. Cut the okra into bite-size pieces. In a bowl, lightly salt the okra and cover with buttermilk. Set aside in the fridge for 1 hour to tenderize okra. In a separate bowl, mix cornmeal, flour, salt, and pepper. Drain okra from buttermilk then dredge okra into cornmeal, rolling around to coat. Place in a deep fryer or frying pan with oil until browned and crisp. Remove okra and drain on a paper towel.

Dahlonega Mint

There was so much gold mined in the area that in 1838 a branch of the United States mint was established in Dahlonega. The other branches were in New Orleans and Charlotte, North Carolina, with the parent mint located in Philadelphia. The mint's records showed that over $6,000,000 worth was coined in Dahlonega until the break out of the Civil War in 1861.

Coins produced at the Dahlonega Mint bear the "D" mint mark and the dates 1838-1861, from which the mint produced coins yearly. The $5.00 half eagle was the first coin produced at the mint in April of 1838. The different coins included the $1.00, $2.50 quarter eagle, $3.00 (only in 1854), and the $5.00 half eagles.

Upon the outbreak of the American Civil War, the Confederate soldiers seized the mint, and it is believed that some gold coins and half eagles were minted under the Confederate State Government. Approximately 1,600 1861 half eagles were struck, but the exact amount is unknown.

A set of Dahlonega coins could total 58 pieces: 24 half eagles, 20 quarter eagles, 1 three dollar pieces, and 13 one dollar pieces. However, 61 coins complete the set if both varieties of the 1846-D and 1842-D are included. (Gold Rush Gallery for information about the different sets of coins)

Because of their relatively low mintage, all Dahlonega-minted gold coins are rare. The "D" mint mark is used today by the Denver mint, which opened in 1863 as an assay office and in 1904 converted into a working mint that is still in operation today producing over 50 million coins daily.

The discovery of gold in California in 1848 caused a decline in the gold production in the area and was plans of abolishing the mint in Dahlonega. During the war the machinery became injured from the exposure and unfit for further use as a mint. Federal soldiers occupied the mint and turned it into a barracks for quartering the soldiers. They closed the mint in 1861 and Congress donated the land to the trustees of the North Georgia College for the purpose of education. In 1878 the old Dahlonega Mint burned to the ground. A new building for the college was built on the original mint location and named after the college founder, William Price, Price Memorial. The gold steeple topping the building is a reminder of the gold minted there.

Image courtesy of AccessNorthGa.com
and coinnews.net

Smith House
Turnip or Collard Greens

1 large bunch of fresh turnip or collard greens
1 teaspoon of salt
¼ teaspoon pepper
¼ pound of salt pork
¼ cup of sugar
Water or chicken broth

Greens should be thoroughly washed free of grit. Remove tough stems. Put greens in a heavy pot. Cover with water, and add salt pork. Bring meat and water to a boil. Add greens and sugar and bring to a hard boil, then lower heat and cook slowly for 1 hour, or until tender. The water should reduce to about a cup. Young greens may not as long to cook. More seasoning may depend upon the greens if they are bitter.

Smith House
Lima Beans

1-16 ounce pack frozen lima beans or 4 cups of fresh shelled lima beans
1-16 ounce can of chicken broth
1 medium onion
2 tablespoons butter
¼ teaspoon salt
¼ teaspoon pepper

In a large sauce pan, melt butter and sauté onions over medium heat until softened. Pour in chicken broth and bring to a boil. Add lima beans, salt and pepper then reduce heat to low and simmer for 30 minutes until the beans are tender.

Smith House

Breads

Thelma Welch, Operator and Owner of The Smith House from 1946-1980

Thelma & Fred Welch

Thelma Ray Welch devoted almost 40 years of her life providing meals for groups and travelers to the area. She was always praised as being a hard-worker and always being the first one on call in time of need.

She always found time for her family and friends. She and Fred were the first to respond to a person's need in time of sickness or sorrow. It is said that they have carried more food to people in Lumpkin County than anyone else. She was a devote Christian and loved her church, Friendship Baptist Church and would regularly announce in church for all the members to come have Sunday lunch with her at the Smith House. During revivals, she made a point to feed all visiting preachers and their family at the restaurant.

She was raised on a farm with eleven other siblings. Her father told Fred when he asked her hand in marriage that he reluctantly gave her away because she was the best hand he had. She took her passion into their marriage and never took a job lightly. During the war, she and Fred went to Akron, Ohio to build planes. She was promoted on every job assignment and moved up in responsibilities. She was well compensated for her work and soon after the war, the couple returned to Dahlonega to start a new life together.

Mr. Fry had purchased the Smith House and needed a hard working team to run the restaurant. With Fred's restaurant experience and her passion for work, they outgrew the little upstairs dining room and expanded into the basement.

She always found time to plant a huge garden for the restaurant and reached out to other farmers when supplies were needed. She soon introduced a variety of plants in her garden and was known as the woman who could grow any plant she put in her garden.

I remember being at my grandmother's house and she would come around the corner headed to her kitchen carrying a bushel of different vegetables that was sat on her door step. I would ask who gave them to her and she would only say "I don't know but only God knows." There was a secret society back then of growers that always shared their bounty with other farmers. Sharing was a part of her life and as a child this character was in-graved in the person that I have become.

Fred continued to work in the kitchen until his death on February 1, 2005, at the age of 89. Thelma worked full-time in her garden until her death on February 4, 2011, at the age of 88.

Even after her passing is remembered as being such a fine Christian woman who shared her beliefs and passion with everyone she met.

Fred & Thelma's engagement

Smith House Yeast Rolls
by Thelma Welch

- 1 package yeast
- 1½ cups lukewarm water
- 2 eggs (unbeaten)
- 4 tablespoon sugar
- 1 teaspoon salt
- ¾ cups Wesson oil
- 4 ½ cups plain flour

Dissolve yeast in lukewarm water. Add all other ingredients, mixing flour last. Make a soft dough. Knead lightly-set aside in a warm place and let rise until size doubles. Punch dough down and let rise a second time. Roll out on a floured surface, cut with a roll cutter (or biscuit cutter). Dip roll into melted butter and fold over. Place on a greased sheet pan. Let rise again 30-35 minutes. Bake at 400° for 10 minutes, or until lightly brown.

Smith House Corn Muffins
by Fred Welch

- 2 cups self-rising corn meal
- 2 tablespoons flour
- 1 cup buttermilk
- 1 large egg, beaten
- 1 tablespoon shortening or vegetable oil

Preheat oven to 450° and add skillet with shortening or oil until ready. Whisk egg and buttermilk in a bowl. Add cornmeal and flour to buttermilk and mix until smooth. Take skillet out of oven and pour mixture and bake at 450° for 25-30 minutes.

Thelma's Hospitality

Spring of 1963, a competition was held by the National Chamber of Commerce to beautify North Georgia. Northerners coming through only saw the area as just a pass through to Florida. North Georgia Representatives wanted a different look and promote a travel destination for visitors. A 6-month clean-up project was underway and a competition was held between counties by size according to population to win the grand prize of the most beautiful town in North Georgia. Forty counties stepped up to the challenge and Dahlonega was in population Class IV (2,500-10,000) with thirteen other counties. Massive clean-up was underway supervised by the local Chamber of Commerce and Jaycees. Appointed chairman for four areas of interest were announced: Clean-Up and Beautification, Accommodations and Facilities, Points of Interest, and New Attractions. Thelma stepped up to the challenge and on the day before the judging she invited the judges to stay the night in the inn and also hosted a banquet in their honor. She invited local citizens to attend the banquet so they would be impressed with Dahlonega's "Southern Hospitality". The local newspaper ran an ad to invite all who could come to the restaurant for a look into the future of tourism in this small town. She cooked her finest recipes from her collection and also Ms. Bessie Smith famous fried chicken recipe. She served her buttermilk biscuits recipe and the judges fell in love with her cooking and immediately gave an impressive first impression of the local heritage. The next morning they took to the streets touring business and the finely combed public square. They visited the other towns but not surprisingly, Dahlonega took 1st place in Class IV in the "Stay and See" Georgia contest (see pages 86 & 87). The award ceremony was to be hosted at the famous Dinkler Plaza in Atlanta Georgia at a luncheon on May 30, 1963. Tickets were sold to the event for $2 and all personnel in the tourism industry were present along with other state representatives. Thelma's biscuits won such an impression that she was invited to the Dinkler Plaza to cook her buttermilk biscuit recipe for a breakfast in honor of the state legislators attending the event. She and her valuable employee, Doris Abee joined with the chefs of the Dinkler to cook an outstanding breakfast. They joined in with our local Chamber of Commerce and Jaycees, Madeline Anthony, and Mr. Fry (who at that time owned the Smith House) to attend the award ceremony.

Winning the state "Stay and See" award started a huge market for tourism in Dahlonega that has successfully thrived for fifty years and is continuing on for the next generation of tourism.

Left to right: Thelma Welch, employees of Dinkler, and Doris Abee

Left to right: Doris Abee, head cook at Dinkler, and Thelma Welch

Angel Biscuits
by Thelma Welch

- 1 package yeast
- 2 tablespoons lukewarm water
- 1 teaspoon baking soda
- 3 teaspoons baking powder
- 5 cups plain flour
- 2 tablespoons sugar
- 1 teaspoon salt
- 1 cup shortening
- 2 cups buttermilk

Dissolve the yeast in warm water. Combine flour, baking soda, baking powder, salt, and sugar. Cut in shortening until it becomes the size of peas. Add buttermilk and then yeast mixture. Stir until flour is dampened. Knead on floured surface. Roll out and cut into biscuits. Bake at 400° for 8-10 minutes. If preparing dough ahead, cover tightly with plastic wrap and store in refrigerator.

Sweet Potato Biscuits

- 1 cup all-purpose flour
- 3 teaspoons baking powder
- 2 teaspoons white sugar
- 1 teaspoon salt
- 2 tablespoons shortening
- ¾ cup mashed sweet potatoes
- ¼ cup milk

Preheat oven to 400°. In a medium bowl, sift flour and add baking powder, sugar and salt. Cut in shortening until pieces are pea-sized or smaller. Add sweet potatoes and milk until mixture makes a soft dough. Roll down onto a floured surface and into a ½ inch thickness. Cut biscuits with a cutter or round object and place biscuits 1 inch apart on a greased baking sheet. Bake for 12-15 minutes or until golden brown.

William Benjamin Fry, Owner of the Smith House from 1946-1970

It's 5 o'clock Somewhere

In 1946, William Fry purchased the Smith House at five o'clock in the morning. It all started one evening when Mr. Fry and Mr. Smith discussed a business proposition about purchasing the property. Wanting to sleep on the idea, Mr. Fry went home thinking about the deal. He went to bed tossing and turning, and at 4:30 a.m. he was back at the owner's door. The deal was closed at 5:00 a.m. William Fry had more projects than time, so he contacted Fred and Thelma Welch to run his dining room in the upstairs portion of the house. Dining room operations were later moved to the basement, where the Welches lived in a room behind the kitchen. They soon became famous for serving platters of food on the long tables, where customers help themselves and pass a platter to their neighbor. The Welches continued the family-style tradition Bessie Smith started in the 1920s.

Mr. Fry would take Smith House guests to local mines and show them how to pan for gold. If persuaded, he would take them to visit his favorite fishing holes. Mr. Fry helped put Lumpkin County on the map as a tourist attraction because of its gold history. He entertained visitors with his tales of gold rush days and demonstrations of gold-panning. His passion for gold panning was handed down from his father, Bill Fry, who arrived in North Georgia in the late 1880s to be the superintendent of Crown Mountain Mining Company. Fry's father was instrumental in the development of the first gold museum, located on Crown Mountain, and served as president of the Chamber of Commerce. He worked closely with the Dahlonega Jaycees on the project to collect gold for the Capitol Dome and accompanied the three-day journey in wagon trains to Atlanta. Proudly he presented the gold to Governor Griffin on that historic day in Atlanta.

Mr. Fry would answer any question by telling stories and saying: "I'm gonna tell you, but first I'm gonna tell you somethin' else, and that somethin' else I'm gonna tell you will lead right back to what I'm gonna tell you."

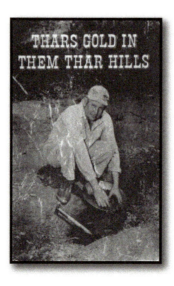

Smith House Cinnamon Rolls

Use Smith House yeast roll recipe

1 stick of melted butter
2 cups of brown sugar
2 tablespoons cinnamon
1 teaspoon nutmeg

Preheat oven to 350°. Roll out dough with a floured rolling pin, until it has an oblong shape. Take melted butter and brush top of the dough. Mix together brown sugar, cinnamon, and nutmeg. Sprinkle mixture over dough. Start at one end and roll dough to look like a log. Pinch the end of the dough so it will not unroll. Flip the dough so the pinched end is placed on the counter. Take a knife and cut into 2-inches pieces. Place parchment paper on a baking sheet and lightly spray with oil. Place rolls on the sheet and bake at 350° for 15 minutes, or until browned.

Smith House Sausage Rolls

Use Smith House yeast roll recipe

1 pound of ground sausage
1 pack softened cream cheese
1 cup shredded cheese (sharp or cheddar)

Preheat oven to 350°. Cook sausage in a fry pan until done. Thoroughly drain sausage and set aside. Roll out dough with a floured rolling pin until it has an oblong shape. Spread cream cheese on dough giving a even layer. Spread sausage and cover with a thin layer of cheese. Start at one end of the dough and roll to look like a log. Pinch the end of the dough so it will not unroll. Flip the dough so the pinched end if on the counter. Take a knife and cut into 2 inch pieces. Place parchment paper on a baking sheet and lightly spray with oil. Place rolls on the sheet and bake at 350° for 15 minutes or until brown.

Effie Kate Fry

Effie & Bill Fry

Bill and Effie Fry were owners of the Smith House from 1946-1970. Effie enjoyed spending time with Thelma Welch, creating new and reviving old recipes for the family style menu. They worked together on crafting the famous yeast roll recipe that is still served today. The women also cooked Mr. Fry's favorite cornbread, which they named "Lacy Cornbread" because it looked lacy while it was frying. Thelma looked up to Effie as an inspirational and Godly influence in her life. A deeply religious woman, Effie was a devout Christian committed to reading her bible daily.

She was loyal to the Dahlonega Baptist Church for fifty years and taught Sunday school every week. She was also the director of vacation bible school. Effie supported and assisted in the girl's auxiliary and the mission at the church. Effie was instrumental in the public affairs of Dahlonega and kept civic awards in perspective. She was an active member in the local PTAs and women's clubs at church. Mr. and Mrs. Fry were awarded the titles of Gold Rush King and Queen in 1974. She devoted a great deal of her time to helping others and serving God, not only in church, but also in her life, home and community.

Bill Fry's Lacy Cornbread

½ cup of white cornmeal (stone ground preferred)
¼ teaspoon salt
2 tablespoons water
¼ cup bacon dripping or 2 tablespoons oil

Combine cornmeal, salt, and water in a mixing bowl. In a cast iron skillet, heat 2 drippings or oil over medium heat. When pan is hot, take a tablespoon and spread mixture (similar to a pancake) from center outward. The mixture will then look lacy and bubbly. Cook approx. 3 minutes or until edges are brown Turn with an egg turner to the other side and cook until golden brown. Repeat steps until batter is finished adding more oil when needed.

Crackling Corn Bread

1 ½ cups corn meal
1 teaspoon salt
2 tablespoons flour
½ teaspoon baking soda
1 egg, beaten
1 cup buttermilk
1 ½ cups cracklings (fried pork skin)
1 tablespoon shortening or oil

Preheat oven to 425°. Place skillet with oil or shortening in oven until ready. Bring water to a boil in a small saucepan and add cracklings. Cook cracklings for 5-8 minutes until done. Sift corn meal, flour, and baking soda together. Whisk eggs and buttermilk together then add to dry ingredients. Mix well and add cracklings. In skillet, add mixture and bake at 425° for 25-30 minutes. Remove from oven and take a plate and cover skillet and flip to release cornbread.

Buttermilk

There was once a small pasture area where locals could keep their animals behind the Smith House. Mr. Couch, a local ordinary man, owned a certain cow named Bessie that he would daily fetch from the small pasture and walk home. He would walk her up the road behind the Smith House where Freddy Welch (owner of the Smith House 1970-present), as a young boy, would be shucking corn on the back porch. Freddy would yell to him "Moo-Cow," so Mr. Couch would refer to Freddy each time he saw him as "Moo-Cow." He crossed the street in front of the Smith House and went down Park Street where he lived to milk Bessie for his evening milk. Locals would recall him singing *"Bringing in the Sheaves"* to the cow as they walked.

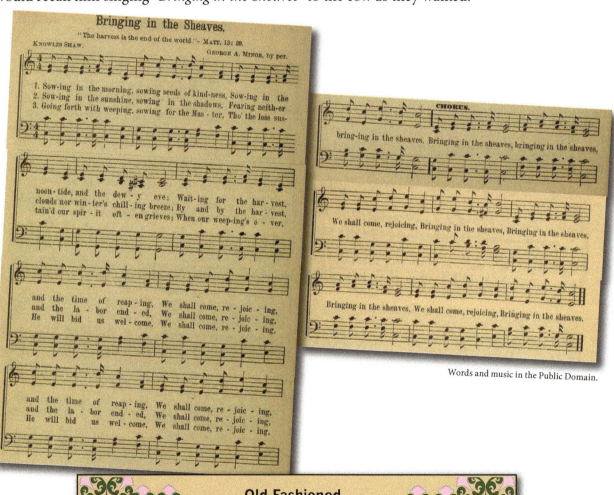

Words and music in the Public Domain.

Old Fashioned Buttermilk Pie

1 9-inch pastry crust
2/3 cup buttermilk
2 cups sugar
1 tablespoon flour
½ cup butter, melted
1 teaspoon vanilla

Preheat oven to 375. Line a 9-inch pie plate with pastry. In a mixing bowl, beat eggs until smooth. Add buttermilk and mix well. Add sugar, flour, butter, and vanilla. Blend well. Pour into pastry-lined plate. Bake in oven for 1 hour, or until knife inserted in center comes out clean.

Smith House Cornbread Dressing

- 4 cups cornbread crumbled
- 2 cups bread crumbs (yeast rolls, white bread or biscuits)
- ½ cup of celery chopped
- Salt and Pepper to taste
- 6 cups of chicken broth (may substitute turkey or vegetable)
- 3 eggs beaten
- 2 teaspoons poultry seasonings
- ½ teaspoon sage
- 1 medium onion chopped
- ½ cup melted butter

Preheat oven to 350°. Cooked chopped onion and celery in 2 cups of water until tender. Cool and set aside. Meanwhile, crumble cornbread and bread crumbs in a separate bowl. In a large bowl, add bread crumbs, eggs, cooled celery and onions, broth, seasonings, and mix together thoroughly. Grease a large casserole dish and pour mixture. Bake for 20 minutes and remove from oven. Top with melted butter and continue cooking for 10 minutes or until brown and crisp on top.

Easy Stuffing

- 1 loaf white bread
- ¾ cup butter or margarine
- ¾ cup finely chopped onions
- 1 cup chopped celery
- ¼ cup chicken broth (may substitute turkey or vegetable broth)
- 1 teaspoon poultry season
- ¼ teaspoon pepper

Tear bread into small pieces and cover with broth. In a large saucepan, sauté onions and celery in butter until tender. Stir in bread and add season. Fill into a cavity of a 12-16 pound turkey and bake until turkey is completely done. Or stuffing can be cooked in a greased casserole dish and bake at 350° for 30-40 minutes.

Thelma's Hospitality — See story on page 78

GEORGIA TRAVEL COUNCIL
Georgia State Chamber of Commerce
1200 COMMERCE BUILDING   ATLANTA 3, GEORGIA

May 7, 1963

Dear Mrs. Anthony,

    We are happy to inform you that your community has been selected as a semi-finalist in the STAY and SEE GEORGIA Program.

    William Hughes, Travel Editor, Cleveland Press
    Mrs. Marge Klein, Travel Editor, Cincinnati Inquirer
    E. Y. Chapin, Pres. Rock City Gardens & Travel Council Chairman
    Glenn Anthony, State Chamber's Public Relations Representative
    Mrs. Mozelle Christian, Manager, State Chamber's Travel Council

will take a three and a half day trip through the State and visit the eleven semi-finalist communities. We will be traveling in a ~~private plane including~~ *an auto* ~~a pilot and co-pilot making a party of seven.~~ *& party will be 5 in number.*

    We expect to be in *Dahlonega on Wednesday May 15th for dinner around 7:30 P.M. lodging & early breakfast on the 16th & tour & depart at 9:30 A.M. on the 16th.*

    We would like to tour your community and see your STAY and SEE GEORGIA projects in action.

    Looking forward to being with you.

        Cordially,

        Ed

        E. Y. Chapin, III, Chairman
        Travel Council

May 7, 1963

TO: STAY and SEE GEORGIA Participants

Thank you for your participation and many fine achievements in the first STAY and SEE GEORGIA program. Enclosed is a list of the semi-finalists and a copy of the Tour Itinerary which will be followed by the judges who will make the decision on the top winners in the five population categories and also name the top 1963 STAY and SEE GEORGIA Town.

This has been a very successful year and we are anticipating even more projects launched and committees activated for the 1963-64 program.

We hope that you will keep up the work started and reap many benefits during this summer's tourist season.

After May 1, 1963	Continue STAY and SEE Projects. These activities can be counted on next year's program.
May 12 - 16	Travel Editors tour the semi-finalists in each population category with Chamber representatives
May 20 - 24	Top Winners in the five population categories will be announced.
May 30, 1963	STAY and SEE GEORGIA Luncheon 12:15 P.M. Dinkler-Plaza Sponsor: Atlanta Junior Chamber of Commerce

The five winners will be asked to attend and present a two and a half minute speech on "What the STAY and SEE GEORGIA program has meant to my community".

State winner will be announced.

All STAY And SEE GEORGIA participants and interested parties are invited to attend. There will be a $2.00 luncheon charge. See Order Form enclosed.

The Atlanta Journal   Friday, May 17, 1963

EDITOR SAYS
Georgia's Tour Image Is Changing

FORSYTH, Ga. (UPI) — A veteran travel editor says Georgia is beginning to overcome the image long held by Northern tourists — namely, that it is merely a place to pass through en route to Florida.

But although the state is "on the move," Cleveland Press writer William Hughes said Thursday that much remains to be done by the individual communities.

Hughes noted that Georgia had long suffered "speed trap and fee system law enforcement stigmas" which damaged the state's tourist potential.

Hughes and Miss Marge Klein, travel editor of the Cincinnati Enquirer, concluded a four-day tour of the state Thursday to select a top tourist town.

The writers looked at 11 communities, selected as semifinalists from 40 entries in the Georgia State Chamber of Commerce travel council-sponsored Stay-and-See-Georgia tourist promotion contest.

The two judges visited Columbus, Chatham County, Bartow County, Glynn County, Macon County, Thomasville, Dahlonega, Monroe County, Washington, Jefferson and Pine Mountain.

The grand winner and winners in five population categories will be announced May 30 at a meeting of the Atlanta Junior Chamber of Commerce.

"Thanks to the enthusiastic response to this program," said Hughes, "I have found throughout Georgia that the state is beginning to replace the Northern image of its being just a place to pass through on the way to Florida."

Miss Klein and Hughes were accompanied by state chamber officials and E. Y. Chapin, president of the Rock City Gardens.

---

6 THE ATLANTA CONSTITUTION, Friday, May 17, 1963

Travel Editors End State Tour To Select Top Tourist Town

Constitution State News Service

FORSYTH — Two newspaper travel editors and three Georgia State Chamber of Commerce officials concluded here Thursday a four-day tour of the state to select Georgia's top tourist town. They looked at 11 communities, selected as semi-finalists from 40 entries in the Chamber Travel Council-sponsored "Stay and See Georgia" tourist promotion contest.

The judges, Bill Hughes of the Cleveland Press and Marge Klein of the Cincinnati Enquirer, visited Columbus, Chatham County, Bartow County, Glynn County, Macon County, Thomasville, Dahlonega, Monroe County, Washington, Jefferson and Pine Mountain.

Accompanying the two veteran travel writers were travel council chairman E. Y. Chapin, president of the Rock City Gardens; council manager Mozelle Christian, and chamber public relations manager Glenn Anthony.

The grand winner and winners in five population categories will be announced May 30 at an Atlanta Junior Chamber of Commerce luncheon at the Dinkler Plaza Hotel.

"Through the efforts of programs such as the one just completed, I am confident that Georgia will soon replace the Northern image of being just a place to pass through on the way to Florida," Hughes said.

He added that "too long has Georgia been hampered by speed traps and fee-system law enforcement; however, I think the state is on the verge of really blossoming into an excellent tourist state."

Hughes, who travels extensively throughout the United States and Europe, reminded that "much remains to be done and it will not be easy and it will not be cheap."

The Dahlonega Nugget
May 31, 1963

We congratulate Mrs. Jessie Garner and all the members of her committee upon winning the "Stay and See" Georgia contest in Dahlonega's population division.

"Our Town" shows the results of the efforts Mrs. Garner and the committee made.

Fifty local Dahlonega and Lumpkin County citizens showed appreciation for the work of the committee by attending the dutch dinner for the judges held at the Smith House. At the dinner, enthusiasm was shown for many projects for the next contest.

That's Dahlonega — even before the winner is announced, leaders in community projects have launched forth with plans for another year!

Stay and See Judges To Get Dahlonega Meal

DAHLONEGA — Everyone is invited to attend a dinner at the Smith House in Dahlonega Wednesday in honor of Stay and See Contest judges.

The judges will be in Dahlonega and tour the town and view its accomplishments under the State Chamber of Commerce sponsored program to clean the face of Georgia.

A party from the State Chamber in Atlanta will be touring with the judges.

Dahlonega is one of 11 state semi-finalists in the contest. Winners in five categories will be announced May 17. The state winner will be named on the 30th in Atlanta at an Atlanta Jaycee banquet.

a Nugget

DAHLONEGA, GEORGIA, FRIDAY, MAY 10, 1963

Dahlonega In Running for Award In "Stay, See Georgia" Campaign

The "Stay and See" Georgia beautification contest is drawing near an end. Dahlonega has made a grandstand play for the championship award in this contest launched by the State C of C.

For many weeks now, leaders, citizens, businessmen and civic organizations have worked hard and continuously toward beautifying our town, and they have accomplished a great deal.

Their labors are bearing fruit. Dahlonega is ranking in the top three in our population class in the state, along with Washington and Jefferson. Judging is based on actual accomplishments of the town in making the community more attractive.

We had until May 1 to work on this project — and work we did. For that matter, we still are.

The entire county and city have reason to be proud, and soon now, the final judging.

Five judges will visit us next Wednesday and Thursday, May 16 and 17, and will evaluate our efforts.

Mr. William Hodges, Travel Editor of the Cleveland Press; Mrs. Marge Klein, Travel Editor of the Cincinatti Enquirer; E. Y. Chapin, President of Rock City Gardens and Travel Council Chairman; Glenn Anthony, State C of C Public Relations Representative; and Mrs. Mozelle Christian, Manager of the State Chamber Travel Council; will leave Jeferson around 5:30 Wednesday and hope to be her by 7:30.

A dutch supper will be held at the Smith House upon their arrival.

Thursday between 7:30 and 9:30 a. m. the judges will decide our fate. The entire county and residents of Dahlonega are urged to meet the judges at the Smith House Wednesday night at 7:30. Make your reservations for supper before noon Tuesday, May 15.

Dahlonega Makes Finals Of Stay and See Contest

DAHLONEGA — Dahlonega is one of five finalists in the Georgia State Chamber of Commerce Stay and See Georgia contest.

Winners from five divisions were selected by travel editors William Hughes of the Cleveland Free Press and Marge Klein of the Cincinatti Enquirer. The overall state winner will be announced May 30 in Atlanta.

Georgia towns and counties entering the contest were divided, according to population, into five categories. Dahlonega competed in the 2,500 to 10,000 population class and competed against Forsyth and Washington in the semi-finalist stages of the contest. There were 14 entries in Dahlonega's category when the contest began.

Division winners were selected on the basis of projects completed. Dahlonega was involved in four projects — beautification and cleanup-accommodations and facilities-points of interest and new attractions committees, the latter two projects were combined under a tourist committee.

The grand winner of the Stay and See Contest will be announced at an Atlanta Junior Chamber of Commerce Luncheon, May 30 at the Dinkler Plaza Hotel.

Winners of the other four categories were Columbus, class one, over 60,000 — Bartow County, class two, 25,000 to 60,00 — Macon County and Thomasville, (a tie) class three, 10,000 to 25,000 — (Dahlonega) — and Pine Mountain, class four, under 2,500.

Jefferson was a semifinalist in class four.

The Stay and See Georgia contest is a grass roots movement to clean the face of Georgia and prepare for the tourist. Travel editor Hughes said he believes "this program is obviously going to increase the tourist trade in Georgia . . .and erase the Northern image that Georgia is just a state to pass through on the way to Florida."

Smith House

Beverages

Southern Table Wine

Southerners have been drinking sweet tea cold since the early 1800s. The first tea plant arrived in the country during the late 1700s by French explorers. The original tea was made with green tea, not black, and was called punches. Black tea replaced green as the preferred tea for serving cold.

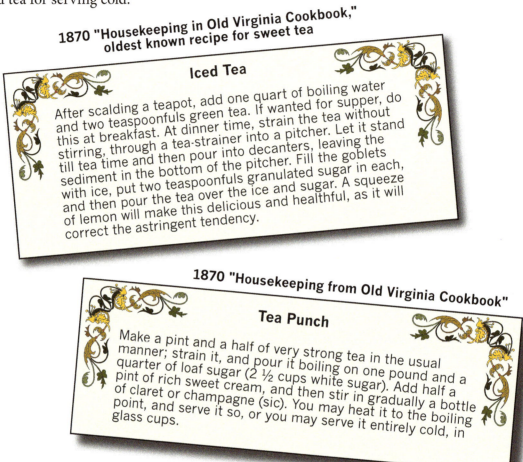

1870 "Housekeeping in Old Virginia Cookbook," oldest known recipe for sweet tea

Iced Tea

After scalding a teapot, add one quart of boiling water and two teaspoonfuls green tea. If wanted for supper, do this at breakfast. At dinner time, strain the tea without stirring, through a tea-strainer into a pitcher. Let it stand till tea time and then pour into decanters, leaving the sediment in the bottom of the pitcher. Fill the goblets with ice, put two teaspoonfuls granulated sugar in each, and then pour the tea over the ice and sugar. A squeeze of lemon will make this delicious and healthful, as it will correct the astringent tendency.

1870 "Housekeeping from Old Virginia Cookbook"

Tea Punch

Make a pint and a half of very strong tea in the usual manner; strain it, and pour it boiling on one pound and a quarter of loaf sugar (2 ½ cups white sugar). Add half a pint of rich sweet cream, and then stir in gradually a bottle of claret or champagne (sic). You may heat it to the boiling point, and serve it so, or you may serve it entirely cold, in glass cups.

I can visualize the first pioneers here in Dahlonega sitting on their front porches on a hot summer day with an ice-cold glass of sweet tea. In some cultures, a bottle of wine is on the table, but in the South, a ready pitcher of tea accompanies dinner. There are two types of tea: sweetened and un-sweetened. Over the past few years there has been an increase in sweet tea sales in fast food and casual dining restaurants over its counterpart, soda.

There are two ways to make the southern delight: either by boiling water in a sauce pan or brewing water in a coffee pot with tea bags. Sugar is preferred over other sweeteners.

Tips for making the perfect pitcher of tea

Have a glass or metal pitcher ready. In a sauce pan boil water, add tea bags, and the desired amount of sugar. Let cool and pour into pitcher. Dilute with water and refrigerate.

In a coffee maker, put a tea bag where you normally would add coffee and brew. In a pitcher, add 1 cup of sugar (less or more if desired) and pour brewed tea in a container. Dilute with water and refrigerate until ready to serve. Have freshly cut lemons ready.

Smith House Sweet Tea

3 family-size tea bags
3 cups water
1 cup sugar
7 cups cold water

Bring 3 cups of water to a boil in a saucepan. Add tea bags and boil for 3 minutes. Remove from heat and steep for 10 minutes. Discard tea bags. Add sugar, stir until it is dissolved. Pour into a gallon-sized glass pitcher and add 7 cups cold water. Serve over ice. Have sliced lemons ready to add for extra flavor and freshness! Garnish with mint leaves, if desired.

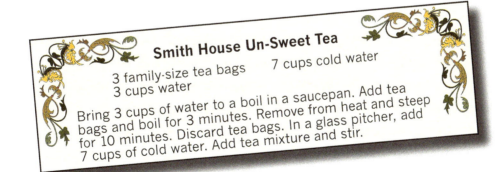

Smith House Un-Sweet Tea

3 family-size tea bags
3 cups water
7 cups cold water

Bring 3 cups of water to a boil in a saucepan. Add tea bags and boil for 3 minutes. Remove from heat and steep for 10 minutes. Discard tea bags. In a glass pitcher, add 7 cups of cold water. Add tea mixture and stir.

The Present Day Smith House

The Smith House is always expanding into new markets. During my grandparents' time of running the operations, they opened the doors to whoever was hungry for a good home-cooked meal. Today, business is different, as we now cater to various markets that offer more challenges.

The charter bus market has always been a dependable and secure business for us. We marketed to these companies back in the 1980s and established relationships that are still solid today. Not only do charter bus companies come throughout the year, but also school field trip groups come to the area to visit our gold mines and learn about Lumpkin County history. On a normal spring day, we could serve over 300 school kids lunch while here on their field trip. We also cater their lunch to Consolidated Gold Mine when they are looking for a quick outside lunch.

One of our bigger markets that has grown in the past eight years is allowing individuals and groups to reserve our private dining rooms. We market to wedding parties to host their rehearsal dinners. When the wedding market expanded in Dahlonega and more venues opened, we responded by increasing the amount of private dinners we served weekly. We received several requests from wedding parties for a full service wedding venue. In the spring of 2015, we renovated the lot adjacent to the Smith House to provide a wedding venue called the Smith House Gardens. We are fortunate to now be able to house the entire wedding party in our historic inn, host their ceremony in our beautiful garden, and serve their dinners throughout the weekend.

In the last few years, our catering business has exploded. Since 2013 we started bidding on smaller outside functions when we found time to host. However, the word spread and in 2015 our catering business has expanded so that we mostly cater weddings at various venues and also functions like family gatherings. We anticipate in the next few years that the catering business will be one of the biggest markets we serve.

Other smaller markets include business, birthday, and retirement parties. We have three beautifully decorated private dining rooms that allow parties to enjoy the privacy and relaxing atmosphere.

Smith House Lemonade

6 lemons, squeezed, making 1 cup juice
½ cup sugar
4 cups of water

Combine the sugar and 1 cup of water in a small saucepan and bring to a boil, stirring until the sugar is dissolved. In a pitcher, combine the sugar mixture with the lemon juice and 3 cups of water. Stir and serve over ice. Garnish with lemons.

The "Arnold Palmer" drink is a favorite drink ordered at the Smith House. The drink is equal parts sweet tea and lemonade.

Smith House Peach Punch

3 peach Jell-O® packets
1 cup sugar
1 can (46-ounce) pineapple juice
1 can thawed lemonade concentrate
2 cups cold water
2 (2-liter) bottles of ginger ale
3 peach-flavored sodas
Fruit: Fresh pineapple, peaches, and cherries (drained and rinsed)

Boil 3 cups of water and then take it off the heat. Add Jell-O® and sugar to the water and stir until the sugar is dissolved. In another large container, pour in lemonade and water; stir and then add pineapple juice, and stir in Jell-O®. In two gallon-sized jars, pour mixture in and place in freezer for 3 hours.

When ready to mix, pour one gallon at a time into a punch bowl and add half of the bottle of ginger ale and one peach soda. Add another batch if your bowl is large enough.

If you prefer to have an ice ring for the bowl: In a Bundt pan add the desired fruit and the liquid from the gallon jars before freezing. Freeze the mold completely, approximately 4-5 hours. Remove from freezer and let sit for 15-20 minutes. Turn mold upside down inside the punch bowl to loosen the ice from the mold. Add the gallon jar of Jell-O®, ginger ale, and soda.

Hint: If using an ice mold, do not freeze the mixture (unless you like it slushy) and keep soda, ginger ale, and Jell-O® mixture in the fridge while waiting for the mold to set.

Wedding on the Waves
Frank and Esther Hall

Frank Wayland Hall purchased a lot off of the public square of Dahlonega to build a grand house for his newlywed wife Ester Caroline Hall. Esther coming from a common family was treated with royalty during her short time with Frank. They married in 1898 and the ceremony took place on Frank's yacht in Palm Springs Florida. He fittingly named the boat after his wife the Ether C. The author of the article (far left) noted a spectacular day for a wedding on the waves. The ceremony was a small with only family friends and his mother present.

Dahlonega folks celebrated the event and an impressive write up in both the local newspaper and The Tropical Sun paper in Palm Springs Florida. The paper reflects on the day as a fitting day for a royal wedding as the yacht departs into the open seas.

Esther and Frank soon returns after spending the cold weather in warmer conditions to oversee the construction of her grand house, present the Smith House. Shortly afterwards, their daughter Frances is born in Esther's grand house.

Dahlonega Nugget, April 8th, 1898 — The wedding of Frank Hall

Wedded on the Waves.

The wedding of the Hon. Frank W. Hall and Mrs. Esther C. Brown yesterday afternoon, took place under circumstances exceptionally novel and beautiful. At 2 o'clock the party sailed away from the wharf in front of Mr. Hall's cluster of elaborate tents that nestle under the great outspreading forest trees at his camp, two miles north of Palm Beach.

The party on board consisted of the bride and groom, the venerable mother of the groom, Mrs. L. C. Hall, Mr. John S. Calkins, of Los Angeles, Cal., the Rev. and Mrs. J. N. Mulford, Mr. L. C. Holmes (who transformed the boat into its new form), Miss Iola Weaver, and John Wilder, skipper.

As they shot by the Riviera Hotel toward Pitts Island, Mr. Mulford alluded in fitting terms to the shapely little craft, and the auspicious occasion and then christened her the "Esther C.," in honor of the bride. He then offered a dedicatory prayer referring to our Lord Jesus who in the days of his earthly pilgrimage, blest with his presence the fishing boat of Simon Peter and Andrew his brother. He spoke of this boat as set apart for the purpose of health, restfulness and recreation. Immediately after this, Mr. Mulford performed the marriage ceremony of the Episcopal Church, in the cabin with doors and windows wide open, in sight of the sea and the white surf leaping high over the beach. The ceremony rendered from memory, impressively and without the use of Prayer Book, was in full keeping with the freeness of the scene, the soft breeze and blue sky and sparkling lake, and the music of the waves around the bow never seemed more in harmony with the spirit of nature, or the joyful dignity of a true marriage.

The "Esther C.," an ideal of snug comfort, was just finished and put in commission yesterday morning. The characteristics of the craft will be found described in another column. But we cannot forbear alluding to her many ingenious appointments: The sliding beds, the long folding table, the compacted cupboard, nook for stove, and niche for water cooler, room-saving lockers, and ample cockpit, all developed under the supervision of the owner.

Mr. Hall has for several winters reresorted to the Lake with a little party of friends. He comes fully equipped for a season of restfulness, and thoroughly enjoys our wonderful winter climate. Mr. Hall is one of the prominent citizens of northern Georgia, and is largely identified with the gold mining interests of that part of the State in the vicinity of Dahlonega, a successful industry established prior to the discovery of gold in California. The substantial service rendered by Mr. Hall in the legislative body of Georgia and in various other responsible positions, has gained him the esteem and confidence of the community where his commanding presence and splendid physique simply passes as the outward token of the intrinsic character within.—The Tropical Sun.

The Smith House 1898

Summer Tea Punch

3 family-size tea bags
1 8-ounce bottle of peach nectar
½ can of thawed lemonade concentrate
½ cup of sugar
1 (2-liter) bottle of ginger ale
1 (1-liter) club soda chilled

In a sauce pan, bring 4 cups of water to a boil; add sugar and tea bags. Boil for 2 minutes and remove from heat; let simmer for 15 minutes. Remove tea bags. In a large container, pour peach nectar, lemonade, and tea; let sit in the fridge for 4 hours. Before serving, add ginger ale and club soda. Garnish with sprigs of mint, if desired.

Strawberry Punch

2 strawberry Jell-O® packets
1 pint of fresh or frozen strawberries
3 cups of water
½ cup sugar
1 can (46-ounce) of pineapple juice
2 (2-liter) bottles of Sprite®

In a blender, add strawberries and one cup of water and mix until blended. In a sauce pan, bring two cups of water to a boil; add Jell-O® and sugar. Turn heat off and stir until dissolved. In a large container, add pineapple juice, strawberries, and Jell-O®; stir. Refrigerate mix for 2 hours. In a punch bowl, add mix and slowly add Sprite®.
Hint: Instead of using an ice mold, take frozen strawberries and add to punch.

Smith House

Relishes and Jellies

The Second Welch Generation

Shirley Seabolt married Freddy Welch, the son of Fred and Thelma, on December 17, 1966. Shirley soon became a crucial part in the building of the business and taking the operations to the next phase of growth. She had many talents and cooking skills that the public soon embraced. The Fry family sold the business to the Welch family in 1970. Fred and Thelma continued to run the business as they had since 1946, but the newer generation wanted to expand the inn and restaurant into different markets. Freddy immediately started constructing plans to build on to the original house. He and Shirley expanded the restaurant seating from 85 people to over 300 seating, and Shirley introduced new recipes to the original menu.

Yummy Squash Relish (Pickles)

The squash relish, which we refer to as squash pickles, is one of the most famous recipes here at the Smith House. It soon became one of the signature dishes that people would drive to Dahlonega to taste. The popularity rose, and the demand was high enough so that Shirley decided to can her relish for customers to enjoy at home or give as gifts. Shirley cans over 6-10 dozen jars of squash relish a week during the harvest season, and it sells out weekly. The Smith House ships the relish all over the country, receiving calls from as far away as Hawaii. Many world travelers come to the restaurant and take a few jars of the squash relish back with them so that they can bring a taste of the South to their families. Every year, Shirley contracts with local farmers to buy their harvest of squash so she can supply the demand of the customers. On a given week, she will cook 50 pounds of squash and 20 pounds of zucchini to make her weekly canning supply. The relish is also served on Thanksgiving Day, along with her homemade cranberry relish.

The Thanksgiving Day dinner has grown substantially over the years, and the Smith House now normally serves over 1,200 people. Freddy and his staff cook over 700 pounds of baked turkey and 600 pounds of fried chicken on that day alone. Thanksgiving is a family affair that requires all of the Welches, alongside the dedicated employees, to work together to pull this day off. People from all over the state and country come to enjoy the signature Thanksgiving dishes of the Smith House.

During the fall season, leaf lookers arrive in the North Georgia Mountains to see breath-taking views of the fall foliage. Therefore, autumn is the busiest time of the year for the Smith House. Charter buses average around six to nine on any given day for lunch; many passengers stock up on their supply of squash relish after enjoying an all-you-can-eat meal at the large family-style tables.

Smith House Squash Pickles
by Shirley Welch

- 3 large yellow squash, sliced ¼ inch thick
- 2 medium zucchini, sliced ¼ inch thick
- 2 large onions, sliced ¼ inch thick
- 1 tablespoon of salt
- 1 small jar chopped pimento, drained and rinsed
- 4 cups sugar
- 3 cups vinegar
- 2 teaspoons celery seed
- 2 teaspoons turmeric
- 2 teaspoons mustard seed

In a large glass container, layer the squash in ice. Cover and let stand for 3 hours or overnight. Drain well. In a large pot, bring vinegar, salt, sugar, celery seed, mustard seed, and turmeric to a boil. Add pimentos, onions, and bell peppers; cook for 5 minutes. When mixture is boiling, add squash and zucchini, coating the vegetables in the juice. Cook for another 5 minutes, until squash starts to curl. Sterilize canning jars and pack the vegetable mixtures in jars, then place lids on jars tightly.

Smith House Cranberry Relish
by Shirley Welch

- 3 6-ounce bags of fresh cranberries
- 3 green apples, peeled and cored
- 1 orange peeled and seeded
- 1 teaspoon cinnamon
- ¼ cup lemon juice
- ½ cup of sugar (can use sugar substitute, adjusting measurements to taste)
- 2 6-ounce boxes of strawberry Jell-O®
- 1 cup boiling water
- 1 can concentrate orange juice

Place washed cranberries and apples in a food processor and pulse. In boiling water, dissolve the strawberry Jell-O® stirring constantly. Add cinnamon, sugar, strawberry Jell-O® and orange juice. Taste to see if more sugar needs to be added. Put in refrigerator and let sit overnight.

Harvest Beets
(Wear kitchen gloves to keep hands from staining.)

- 3 cups of cooked and sliced beets
- ½ cup sugar
- 1 tablespoon cornstarch
- 1 teaspoon salt
- ½ cup apple cider vinegar

To cook beets: wash and scrub 4-5 small beets (removing green leaf and stems) until dirt is removed. Place beets in a saucepan and cover with water about an inch. Bring to a boil on high heat then lower to medium for 35-45 minutes or until tender. Drain and rinse with cold water. The skin of beet will peel right off then slice beets and place in a separate bowl. On the stove top, mix sugar, cornstarch, salt, and vinegar. Stir occasionally. When liquid is clear, add mixture to beets and refrigerate 4-6 hours.

The Welch Family's Third and Fourth Generations

Chris and I were born into the Welch family and have enjoyed all of the luxuries of growing up in the family business. While our parents were building the business into the famous icon it is today, the work consumed our family time, and so we learned quickly to help our parents out when needed. As kids, we spent many days exploring for hidden treasures in the building, not knowing that the biggest treasure was located under the building- a mineshaft containing gold.

I enjoy spending my time building the business and working closely with my parents. I was raised in the restaurant with all of the older women watching me and shaping me to be a fine young lady. Now that I have a family of my own, I trusted in the Smith House family to help raise my son, Evan Bafile, to be a fine young man. He, like his mother, was required to help in whatever capacity the Smith House could use him. There was a day when Evan, at the age of eight, was coming in from school and, after exiting the school bus, was soon tying an apron on and helping in the dining room. The small boy went up to the tables and asked the customers if he could get them anything from the kitchen. The customers were so amazed at this young boy wanting to serve them, and they gave him a big tip and a hug. Evan soon saw that this was a good way to make him some toy money! Today, Evan is much older and helps out in whatever capacity is needed, whether that be in the kitchen cleaning, in the dining room serving, or outside helping with the landscaping. Evan also loves working in the family business and, hopefully, he will continue in his endeavors to grow the business into different markets.

Chris has also worked in the family business throughout his whole life. He and his wife, Jeanne, enjoy traveling to marketing conferences to promote the Smith House. He was instrumental in introducing the Historic Hotels of America to our business, and we have been a proud member of the association since 2006. The Smith House meets all of the rigorous requirements and is listed as one of the smallest properties within the Historic Hotels of America. Chris's children, Lauren and Christopher, are growing up around the Smith House and also spend time in the family business. Hopefully, this upcoming fourth generation of children will be as successful as the former generations.

At this point in history, the second, third, and fourth Welch generations are all working together in the business. Not many family businesses make it this far, but we are living proof that it can be done with hard work and loyalty to each other. The Smith House has been a part of us since 1946, and we plan to continue for much longer.

Second and Third Generation Welch
Left to right:
Chris, Freida, Shirley, Freddy

Bread and Butter Pickles

25 medium cucumbers, sliced
12 small onions
½ cup salt or pickling salt
Ice
1 quart white or apple cider vinegar
4 cups sugar
2 tablespoons mustard seed
1 teaspoons turmeric
1-½ tablespoons celery seed

Slice the cucumbers and onions. Add ice to cover with salt for 3 hours. Drain if needed and add more ice during process. Boil vinegar, add sugar and seasonings. Drain cucumbers and onions and add to vinegar. Heat thoroughly. Refrigerate for several hours and serve cold. If canning, add hot pickles to sterilized jars and process in a water bath. Let jars sit overnight.

Okra Pickles

3-½ pounds small okra pods
5 cloves garlic
5 small fresh hot peppers
4 cups of water
1 pint vinegar
⅓ cup pickling salt
2 teaspoon dill seeds

Pack okra tightly into hot sterilized jars, leaving room for the other ingredients to have ¼-inch headspace. Place a clove of garlic and one hot pepper in each of the jars. Combine remaining ingredients in a medium-sized saucepan; bring to a boil. Pour vinegar mixture over okra. Cover at once with metal lids and tighten. Process in a boiling water bath for 10 minutes.

Muscadine Jelly

3 quarts (5 lbs.) fresh muscadines to make 5 cups of muscadine juice
6 cups sugar
¼ teaspoon cinnamon
1 pack of pectin

Fresh muscadines do require a little more work. Pick through the muscadines and remove any stems; wash well. In a large stockpot, bring 2-½ cups of water to a boil, add muscadines and reduce heat. Cook for 20 minutes and then, with a fork, start smashing the muscadines to release the juice. Strain muscadines. Strain juice again through a colander lined with a damp jelly cloth. Pour juice back into a clean stockpot and bring to a boil for 5 minutes; reduce heat. To the muscadine juice add sugar, pectin and cinnamon. The juice should start thickening. At this point, have the sterilized jars ready. Boil hard for 1 minute. Skim foam off. Pour the mixture into jars. Seal the jars and let it sit overnight.

The Art of Canning

Canning is a process that goes back early into history, when the French were running into a problem with keeping food supplies full for their armies during the late 18th century. The military was offering a prize to anyone who could solve their problem of food spoilage. Nicholas Appert studied the concept of bottled wine, and after fifteen years of experimentation found that food properly heated and sealed in airtight containers would not spoil. Tests performed on the French navy in 1806 were successful. A prize of 12,000 francs was awarded to Appert in 1810 for his invention of canning.

An Englishman, Peter Durand, took the concept of canning a step farther when he developed a method of sealing food into airtight tin containers. The demand for canned foods increased with world expeditions and population growth. Bryan Dorkin and John Hall set up the first commercial canning factory in England in 1813. Thomas Kensett, who immigrated to the United States, established the first U.S. canning facility for oysters, meats, fruits, and vegetables in New York in 1812. The whole idea of canning is to limit the growth of microorganisms which cause food spoilage. The original process developed by Appert and Durant has not changed from heating foods with steam and pressure to the temperature of 240-250°F (116-121°C) and sealing into airtight containers.

Today, we mostly rely on commercial factories to process canned foods. However, many gardeners use the canning process during their bounty season to preserve their fresh fruits and vegetables. The process is simple but time consuming. The popping sound of the sealing process goes on for hours while the hot liquid cools inside the jars. This joyful sound is the canner's reward for the hours of hard work.

The Canning Process

Boil 4 cups of water in a large bath canner, add clean glass jars, lids, and rings (always use new). Remove lids and rings with a sterile ladle and place on a clean towel to drain. Add glass jars and boil for 5 minutes, then remove with the sterile ladle and place on a towel to drain. Always use clean and sterilized items when canning.

There are two canning methods: water bath canning and pressure canning.

Water bath canning: Best to use with high-acid foods. Great for jellies, jams, and relishes.

How to: Use the sterile canning jars and add prepared food, leaving headspace at the top of jar. Never fill the jar to the top (typically to the neck of the jar). Clean the rim of the jar and put lid and ring on tightly. Repeat process until finished with all sterile jars. Bring water in a large pot to a boil and add sealed glass jars; boil according to the processing time on the recipe. Remove jars from pot and let sit on counter for 12-24 hours. Make sure all water is wiped from lids. A popping noise will be heard for the entire sealing process from each jar. After 12-24 hours, press the middle of the lid down and it should not flex up and down. If the jars are not sealed, pour out the contents and possibly start again.

(Continued on page 106)

Strawberry Jam

5 cups of fresh strawberries, washed and stemmed

7 cups of sugar
4 tablespoons of lemon juice
1 box pectin

In a separate bowl, crush strawberries to make 4 cups of mashed berries. In a saucepan, mix together the strawberries, sugar, pectin, and lemon juice. Stir over low heat until the sugar is dissolved. Increase the heat to high and bring mixture to a boil, stirring constantly. Transfer mixture to the sterile jars, leaving ¼ to ½ inch headspace, and seal. Process in a water bath.

Moonshine Jelly

5¼ cups of sugar
½ teaspoon of margarine

3 cups of white wine or white grape juice
1 box of pectin

In a pot bring sugar, margarine, wine, and pectin to a boil, stirring constantly. Skim off all of the foam from mixture. Pour the mixture into clean and sterilized glass pint jars. Screw on lids on all jars and process in a water bath. Remove and place on a clean towel with lids up until sealed.

Blueberry Jelly

3-½ cups of blueberry juice (can use blackberry)
5 cups sugar

2 tablespoons lemon juice
1 box of pectin

To make the juice, boil fruit until softened and strain with a cheese cloth. In a sauce pan, add juice, sugar, and lemon juice; bring to a boil. Stir pectin into juice. Bring to a full boil over high heat, stirring constantly for one minute. Remove from heat. Quickly skim off foam and pour into jars, 1/8 inch from top. Quickly seal. Process in a water bath and remove to sit on a clean towel while processing.

The Canning Process (continued from page 104)

Pressure canning: This method heats the contents to 240°, eliminating the risk of food-borne bacteria.

How to: Use the sterile canning jars and add prepared food, leaving headspace at the top of jar. Never fill the jar to the top (typically to the neck of the jar). Clean the rim of the jar and put lid and ring on tightly. Place jars in a canner. Close vent and gradually adjust heat to achieve and maintain recommended pound pressure according to the recipe. Cool pressure canner by removing from heat. Do not remove the weighted gauge. Let canner stand undisturbed until pressure returns to zero. Wait 10 minutes before removing jars and set upright on a clean towel to prevent jar breakage. Leave on towel for 12-24 hours. Make sure water is wiped from lids. A popping noise will be heard for the entire sealing process from each jar. After 12-24 hours, press the middle of the lid down and it should not flex up and down. If the jars are not sealed, pour out the contents and possibly start again.

Canning with Jamie

Jamie Seabolt-Musgrove has been cooking her whole life. She is my lifelong friend. We met in the crib at my grandmother's house back in 1970. Literally, we were infants that shared a crib and instantly bonded. Throughout our lives, we have never parted and share so many funny memories of growing up together.

Jamie, my brother, and I always played behind our house growing up. Since we all were family, we lived on the Seabolt family land. The land was handed down from former generations, and my mother's father left her the property beside the land that was handed down to Jamie's family. We were neighbors and practically lived with each other. We roamed the woods always looking for a new adventure. There were many times when our imagination got the best of us, and when we saw a pile of rocks in the woods, we would hide because of the rumors of the Indians scalping the white man for entering their lands.

As we grew older, I spent a lot of time at Jamie's house watching her mother cook. Normally, I would be at the Smith House with the large crowds, watching the cooks serve large quantities. It was nice to see a family serving on a smaller scale. Jamie, like her mother, loved to cook. She would always jump in to help cook the family's dinner. I wanted that same enthusiasm, so one day when I was alone at my house, I wanted to cook something special. I looked in the fridge and all I saw was a pack of hotdogs. I looked at the pack and pondered how to cook it. I called Jamie and her mother picked up the phone, so I asked her how to cook the hotdogs. She laughed and said, "Do you know how to boil water?" This has been a family joke ever since.

Jamie continues cooking from her family's heritage and spends her extra time canning. In the summer months you can find her either selling her canned goods at her roadside stand or at the Dahlonega Farmers Market on the public square. I am honored to include some of her recipes that she loves to cook and share with her friends.

Jamie's Old Timey Chow-Chow Relish

- 3 large heads of cabbage
- 4 large onions, coarsely chopped, finely chopped, or shredded
- 5 or 6 cups finely chopped peppers
- ¾ cup of kosher salt
- 6 cups vinegar
- 4 cups sugar
- 1 ½ tablespoon dry mustard
- 1 ½ teaspoons turmeric
- 1 teaspoon ground ginger
- 1 heaping tablespoon celery seed
- 5 heaping teaspoons mustard seed

Place chopped vegetables in a large bowl and sprinkle with salt. Stir until roughly combined. Let stand 4 to 6 hours in the refrigerator, and then drain off all the liquid. At this point, taste; if the salt is too strong, rinse vegetables.

In a large cooking pot, combine vinegar, sugar, dry mustard, turmeric, ginger, celery seed, mustard seed, and bring to a boil. Reduce the heat and simmer for 10 minutes. Add the vegetable mixture to the vinegar and spice mixture; stir well. Simmer a few more minutes, eventually bringing it to a boil, and then take it off the heat. Get ready for the glass jars at this point. If you cook the mixture much longer it will become mushy.

Pack the hot mixture into clean, heated canning jars, leaving only a 1/8 inch head space at the top. Place hot canning lids and rings on jars, and tighten. Process jars in a boiling water bath for 10 minutes, and then remove from water. Let the jars sit out overnight on the kitchen counter.

Jamie's Hot Pepper Jam

- 2 cups of cider vinegar
- 2 cups of finely chopped Jalapeño peppers (about 25) with seeds for heat and without seeds for a mild flavor
- 5 cups of granulated sugar
- 1 tablespoon lemon juice
- 1 packet of Sure-Jell

Put the chopped peppers in a heavy pot or deep skillet, and turn heat to medium. Put a lid on and sweat the peppers until moisture develops on the lid (5 to 7 minutes), stirring frequently. Once the peppers have cooked a bit, pour in the vinegar and cook for 5 more minutes on medium heat. Now add the lemon juice and the packet of Sure-Jell. Bring to a rolling boil for one minute. Add all of the sugar and stir, bring back to a rolling boil.

Once the jam has come to the boiling point, cook it for at least one total minute. Watch to ensure it does not boil over. Remove from heat and let the bubbling settle down. Notice that on top of the cooked jam is a foamy, congealed surface. Take a spoon and gently skim off the surface of the jam; throw it away. Make sure not to skim off too much of the actual pepper pulp.

Take a measuring cup and dip it into the hot jam. Pour the mixture into hot jars, leaving about a ½ inch head space from the top of jar. Be careful – this liquid is HOT. Clean rims of canning jars and put the lid on top, screwing the rings side down. Now is the time to put them in a hot bath. Arrange them in a great big boiler pan, making sure the jars do not touch and that they are totally submerged in water. Cover the pot and bring the water to a boil. Cook for 10 minutes. Carefully remove the hot jars from the water with tongs and place them on the counter top, either on a towel or board. Do not put them on their side or upside down. Leave them sitting until you hear all the tops POP. This means they are all sealed.

Smith House

Desserts

Who Murdered Mary?

William Manning Smith, owner of the Smith House, 1944-1946

William Manning Smith, a University of Georgia law school graduate and a champion of equal rights, was the defense attorney in one of the most famous trials in Atlanta. He took on Jim Conley, a janitor at the National Pencil Company in Atlanta, as a client for $4.00. Not only did Smith believe that Conley was telling the truth, but he wanted to make sure that plant foreman Frank Leo's high powered lawyers did not run over the man in court. On April 26, 1913, a thirteen-year-old employee, Mary Phagan, had been murdered at the National Pencil Company. The Mary Phagan case gained the media's attention, and Mr. Smith became highly recognized as a renowned trial lawyer. The movie, "The Murder of Mary Phagan" (1988), which received the 1988 Emmy Award for Outstanding Miniseries, and book, "The Murder of Little Mary Phagan" (Sept. 15, 1989, were made after the account. People still scratch their heads, wondering who murdered Mary.

The principal witness, Jim Conley, a black man who worked as a janitor, testified that he saw Mary enter the factory on Saturday a little after noon to collect her weekly wage from Leo Frank, the plant foreman. Shortly afterwards, Leo admitted to Jim Conley that he murdered Ms. Phagan, and they both disposed of the body. However, at the trial, Jim Conley reported that he discovered Phagan's dead body in the bathroom. He stated that Leo Frank asked him to move her body to the basement furnace, where garbage was normally placed before being incinerated. He further stated that Frank offered him $200 to dispose the body in the furnace, but he refused. Instead, he agreed to write the "death notes," pinning rape and strangulation on another factory worker, Newt Lee, who was the factory night watchman and security guard of the factory. Conley's testimony visibly shook the jury, and the prosecution team did not have solid evidence to prove Frank's innocence.

Leo Frank was pronounced guilty and sentenced by hanging in 1915. The sentence of hanging was downgraded to life in prison after court appeals had lost. Concerned for his safety, Frank was sent to Milledgeville Correctional Institute. Jim Conley was also found guilty for being an accomplice in the murder, and he was sentenced to one year on the chain gang.

William Smith, Conley's lawyer, saw that the facts did not line up with what Conley had presented in court. He publicly announced that he felt that Leo Frank did not murder Mary, and that his client was the real murderer. Smith advocated for Frank and made public appeals of his findings. Appeals were also made from Frank to the Supreme Court, but were denied. After the trial, it seemed hopeful for Frank when Smith publicly sided for his innocence. People who once felt that Frank was the murderer questioned themselves with this new idea that was brought forward. When an angry mob found out that the hanging of Frank had been changed to life in prison, they drove to Milledgeville, broke into the jail, took Leo Frank to Marietta's square and hung him. Every attempt to secure his innocence seemed worthless, and the truth lies in the grave. Later in life, Smith suffered from Lou Gehrig's disease, which caused him to lose his speech. In 1949, Smith was on his death bed and wrote to his son, "In articles of death, I believe in the innocence and good character of Leo M. Frank. W. M. Smith."

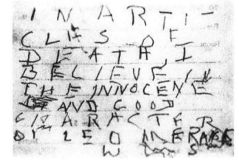

Source: The New York Times, October 04, 1914

Smith House Pumpkin Pie

Pie crust for 9-inch pie
2 eggs
2 cups of mashed cooked pumpkins
¾ cup sugar
½ teaspoon salt
1 teaspoon cinnamon
½ teaspoon ginger
½ teaspoon nutmeg
¼ teaspoon clover
1 cup of brown sugar
1-12 ounce can of evaporated milk

Heat oven to 425°. Beat eggs slightly with rotary beater; beat in remaining ingredients. Pour into the pie crust pan. Bake 15 minutes. Reduce oven temperature to 350° and bake for 35-40 minutes or longer, or until knife inserted between center and edge comes out clean. Cool and serve.

Cooked Pumpkins

Cut pumpkin and clean out seeds and strings. Cut into cubes and cook in a pot of boiling water for 30 minutes. When tender, drain and mash.

Sweet Potato Cake

1½ cups mashed cooked sweet potato
1 egg
⅓ cup of water
1 teaspoon vanilla
⅓ cup of shortening
⅓ cup cooking oil
2 cups sugar
2 cups all purpose flour
¼ teaspoon baking powder
1 teaspoon baking soda
1 teaspoon salt
1 teaspoon cinnamon
1 teaspoon nutmeg
2 cup nuts, chopped fine

Preheat oven to 350°. In a bowl, beat sugar, water, sweet potato, shortening, oil vanilla, and egg. Sift together flour, baking powder, salt, cinnamon and nutmeg. Add dry ingredients to the sweet potato mixture and mix well. Fold in 1 cup of nuts. Pour mixture into three well-greased and floured 9-inch cake pans. Bake at 350° for 45-50 minutes. Cool cake on a wire rack. Place one cake on a serving tray and ice sides and top with a metal spatula. Layer each cake with icing. The top layer sprinkle remaining nuts and refrigerate before serving.

For icing: In a bowl beat 1 (16 ounce) of softened cream cheese and ⅓ cup of softened butter on medium speed until smooth then add 1 tablespoon vanilla and gradually add 3 cups confectioners' sugar and beat on low until smooth.

William and Mary Lou Smith
Owners of the Smith House 1944-1946

In 1944, William and his wife, Mary Lou, moved to Dahlonega with the dream of educating impoverished Appalachian children. They purchased 700 acres of land in the Yahoola valley, nine miles north of Dahlonega, with the intention of becoming Fort Smith Academy. Upon moving to Dahlonega, they purchased the Smith House as their temporary family headquarters and continued the boarding house once established by the former Smiths, Henry and Bessie.

They also acquired The Dahlonega Nugget, the local newspaper. William began voicing his opinion about the upcoming referendum regarding the concern of the free roaming of animals around the public square. His articles concluded with the degrading quality of lifestyle it caused. The town citizens did not agree with Smith's negative responses and they turned their back on him. Mr. and Mrs. Smith sold the Smith House to W.B. Fry in 1946 to continue their dream of Fort Smith Academy.

Smith with prospective students at the Fort Smith School, circa 1946.

Courtesy Walter Smith

Strawberry Pie

- 1 9 inch unbaked pastry shell
- ¾ cup sugar
- 2 tablespoons cornstarch
- 1 cup water
- 1 3 ounce pack strawberry gelatin
- 4 cups sliced fresh strawberries

Preheat oven to 450°. Place aluminum foil over shell and bake for 8 minutes Remove foil and cook for another 5 minutes or until brown.
In a sauce pan, heat sugar cornstarch and water and bring to a boil until thickened. Remove from heat and stir in gelatin. Place in a cool spot.
Wash and stem strawberries. When dry, arrange strawberries in the cooled crust. Pour gelatin mixture over and refrigerate until ready to serve. Before serving, top with Cool Whip®.

Smith House Strawberry Shortcake

- 4 cups of sifted all-purpose flour
- 2 tablespoons baking powder
- 1 teaspoon salt
- ½ cup sugar
- 12 tablespoons cold butter cut into small pieces
- 2 large eggs
- 1 cup milk
- 4 pints of fresh strawberries
- 2 tablespoons of strawberry glaze
- 1 container of Cool Whip®

Preheat oven to 425°. In a round oven pan, grease pan with vegetable oil.

In a large mixing bowl, add flour, baking powder, salt, and sugar. Add cubed butter mix until the mixture has a coarse consistency. In another bowl, add eggs and milk and mix with a fork vigorously until fluffy. Add mixture to the flour and mix for a minute in a pastry mixer. Take mixture and half into each greased pan. Bake in oven for 15 minutes and place on cooling racks.

Meanwhile, wash and cut strawberries in slices removing stems. Mix strawberries with glaze and set aside. Instead of glaze, sugar or sugar substitute can be used on strawberries.

Place cakes on a pretty dish and cover over with strawberries and top with Cool Whip®.

Quick & Easy Strawberry Shortcake

- 1 box yellow cake mix
- 3 large eggs
- ⅓ cup vegetable oil
- ½ cup sugar or sugar substitute
- 2-4 tablespoons sugar or sugar substitute
- 3 pints strawberries, stemmed and sliced
- 1 container Cool Whip®

Heat oven to 350°. Grease and flour two 9-inch round cake pans. In a large mixing bowl, combine the cake mix, eggs, oil, and water that is required on box. Mix well and divide the batter between the two pans. Place in the oven and bake for 30 minutes, or until a toothpick inserted into the center of the cakes comes out clean. Let the cakes cool for at least 10 minutes before removing them from the pans. Cool completely.

Topping: Meanwhile, cut strawberries into slices and sprinkle sugar over them. Put in fridge for 15 minutes, while the cakes are cooling. Place one of the cake layers on a serving platter. Pile on half of the strawberries and half of the whipped cream. Top with the second cake layer, the rest of the whipped cream, and the remaining strawberries. Serve immediately.

Bakery Now Open

The Hope House once was located on the upper parking lot of the Smith House. In 1832, after the completion of the land lottery, the lucky ticket winners claimed their prize. The lot served as a livery stable and was replaced with a fine home in 1845. Harrison Riley built the home with the structure replicating "Georgia Plain Style," which was a two-story house with two rooms per floor. The timber-framed building was surrounded by a plank fence. Riley built many other structures in the town, but this home was the only one to survive. However, he did not reside in the home but used it as a tenant house. Riley sold the home to James Findley, of who Findley Ridge Gold Mine is named after, and he occupied the home until 1859. The next sale was to A.A Hope in 1859, and this is where the building finds its lasting name, the Hope House.

Frank Hall eventually purchased the home as a residence for himself and his new wife, Esther Hall, while their grand home, the Smith House, was being built. Esther did not want to live in the former house of Frank's deceased wife, which was the Hall House, located on the public square of Dahlonega. In 1898, plans to build Esther her dream home began on the spot across from the Hope House.

When the Welch family purchased the Smith House property in 1970, Shirley Welch saw the Hope House as a perfect opportunity to show off her baking skills. She opened a bakery in mid 1980s serving her sugary baked delights in the old home. This venture paid off well for her, and it soon became a favorite spot to satisfy one's sweet tooth. The Hope House became known as The Sugar Shack.

The Hope House was moved in late 1970s to increase needed parking for our inn guest and restaurant patrons. The house still stands today and is located in Auraria, Georgia.

Sketch copied from the Lumpkin County deed records.

Nanny Allene's Strawberry Shortcake

My grandmother, Allene Grizzle or as I referred to her as Nanny Allene, every morning made homemade biscuits, the ole timers called cat head biscuits because they were as large as a cat head, and I would stop by on my way to school and she would hand me out a biscuit wrapped in foil ready for me to eat. She would always make extras so that our Saint Bernard dog would have a biscuit as well. Every morning around 9 a.m. the dog would cross the road headed to Nanny's house for his daily breakfast. In the afternoons, she would take the cold biscuits and have a sweet treat for us with strawberries and sweet cream.

Nanny Allene's Strawberry Shortcake

Biscuit Recipe

- 2 cups self-rising flour
- 2 tablespoons shortening at room temperature
- 1 cup buttermilk
- ½ teaspoon salt

Preheat oven to 400°. Grease a baking sheet and set aside. Sift self-rising flour in a round bowl. Make a round hole in the middle of the flour. Put the shortening in the middle and with a knife cut into pieces then start working into the flour until it looks like coarse crumbs. Slowly add buttermilk while working in the dough. Work into a ball then pinch off pieces and form into round saucer. On greased sheet, place biscuits a few inches apart and bake in oven for 15-20 minutes. Let cool.

Topping

- 1 pint of fresh strawberries, cut into slices
- Sugar
- 1 cup of heavy cream
- 1 teaspoon vanilla, optional

Meanwhile, slice strawberries and sprinkle sugar over them. If using whipping cream, in a cold mixing bowl, add cream and vanilla and with a hand mixer beat until peaks form. Place mixture in fridge until ready to serve.

Cut biscuits in half in a bowl, cover with strawberries and a little juice from strawberries, and top with whipping cream. Whipping cream can be substituted with Cool Whip® or vanilla ice cream.

"Free Jim"

The discovery of gold in 1828 caused many miners to flood the North Georgia Mountains. In 1832 Lumpkin County was surveyed and the lottery-for-land act was enacted. Dahlonega was established as the county seat. James Boisclair, a former slave, came to Dahlonega as a miner, preacher, and entrepreneur. Known as "Free Jim," he contracted with several guardians to purchase his land holdings in Dahlonega, since freed-men were not allowed sole ownership.

Being an entrepreneur, Free Jim opened a bakery on the bottom floor of the courthouse, today the Dahlonega Gold Museum, and with the proceeds purchased the Consolidated Gold Mine. He had recently discovered a vein of gold and desired to buy the lot. He contracted with Dr. Joseph J. Singleton, chief officer of the Dahlonega Branch Mint in 1837, to purchase the lot. He successfully mined the vein and it became known as the "Free Jim Mine." Working the mine for many years made Jim a small fortune and one of the wealthiest merchants in town.

"Free Jim," as seen through the interpretive eyes of artist Don McElliott. There are no known photographs of James Boisclair.

Free Jim's establishment might have resembled the one in this picture.

The proceeds from the mine enabled him to open Dahlonega's largest dry-goods, ice house, and general merchandise store located across the street from present day Smith House. He also established a bar-room which caused much trouble with the Baptist Church of Dahlonega. He was later banned from the church in 1841 for selling liquor on the Sabbath. One year later he was reconciled back with the church.

On February 23, 1836, Free Jim purchased the land across from his successful merchandise store. This land today is known as the Smith House property. He built a structure on the lot where he and another miner live at the time. There are no known pictures of this house but when the present day owners were renovating a portion of the Smith House, they found remains of the foundation.

When the California Gold Rush began in 1849, many of the Dahlonega miners headed west to strike it rich. Free Jim also joined the fortune seekers in late 1850. His passion was mining and would contract with 40-50 miners and receive a portion of their earning and paid their expenses for going. In turn, Free Jim left his land holdings in Dahlonega and relocated to Placer County, California to set up a mining camp and did well for himself. Later moved and established a store, saloon, and boarding house in Sacramento County. However, after years of hard work, his health took a turn for the worse, and he died on October 22, 1861, after a prolonged illness.

Free Jim's Bakery was on the bottom floor of the 1836 Court House Vanishing Georgia, Georgia Archives, University System of Georgia

Free Jim Apple Pie

Pie Crust
- 2 ½ cups all-purpose flour
- 1 ¼ cup of unsalted butter, cut into ½ inch cubes
- 1 teaspoon salt
- 2 teaspoons sugar
- ½ cup sour cream

Egg Wash
- 1 large egg yolk
- 1 tablespoon cream

Apple filling
- 6-8 apples (3 pounds)
- 1 tablespoon lemon juice
- ½ cup sugar
- 3 tablespoons all-purpose flour
- ¼ teaspoon ground allspice
- ¼ teaspoon ground nutmeg
- ½ teaspoon ground cinnamon
- 1 tablespoon brandy
- 1 teaspoon vanilla extract

Preheat oven to 375°.

Apple Filling: Peel and core apples. Cut into quarters and coat with lemon juice to keep from browning. Add brandy and vanilla extract to coat the apples. Combine sugar, flour, and spices in a bowl. Add flour mixture to the apple slices and mix until well coated.

Pie Crust: In a large bowl whisk together 2½ cups of flour, 1 teaspoon salt, and 2 teaspoons sugar. Add the cubed butter and toss with the flour. Work butter into the flour, Continue to work the flour until mixture is wet. Make a well in the center and add sour cream. Separate the dough mixture into two equal piles and work each into a ball. Sprinkle with flour and wrap with plastic wrap and refrigerate for one hour.

Roll out dough into a 12-inch circle (if the dough starts sticking to the rolling pin, add flour) and lay into an empty pie pan. Make sure the dough rolls over the sides of the pan. Mold the dough into the pie pan. Roll the second ball of dough into a 12-inch circle.

Add apple mixture inside the dish and lay the second dough circle on top. Trim excess dough and press sides of dough together with your thumb to make a nice presentation.

Mix the egg yolk and cream together. Use a pastry brush to coat the dough and sides. Use a knife to cut slits in the top of the pie crust for steam to vent.

Cook in an oven at 375°, with a pan underneath to catch drippings, until crust begins to lightly brown, about 20 minutes. Reduce heat to 350° and continue to cook for approximately 45 minutes. Cool and serve! Best with vanilla ice cream.

The Shiners

Dahlonega has hosted many miners and moonshiners in its days. Today, there are documentaries circulating about moonshiners in the North Georgia Appalachian Mountains. Dahlonega cannot be excluded when it comes to moonshining. Making the liquid gold was a favorite pastime of mountain men who were looking for extra ways to pick up on cash, as well as supply their own stock. The distillation was done at night to avoid discovery. Moonshine is typically made with corn mash as the main ingredient, but potato, sugar, and other ingredients can also be used.

Simple everyday ingredients make moonshine: corn meal, sugar, yeast, and water. A simple test for the quality of moonshine was to pour a small amount of it into a spoon and set it on fire. The theory was that a safe distillate burns with a blue flame, but a tainted distillate burns with a yellow flame. Copper stills were most commonly used for brewing. Moonshine is illegally distilled homemade whisky with high alcohol content. In the early years, alcohol consumption was a way for the government to charge high taxes for the product. For this reason, poor farmers built stills in the wilderness at night, working under the light of the moon. Therefore, the drink became known as "moonshine."

I remember as a young girl that when I had a cough the older women gave me a dose of "The Remedy," as they called it, to quiet my nagging cough. "The Remedy" was a mixture of spirits (most commonly used was moonshine), honey, and something sweet so that when taken you would not spit it out. I remember the burning solution going down my throat and killing all the tickle that occurred from playing outdoors as a youngster. After the first teaspoon, I was immediately better and did not want any more. I think that mothers would have a little jar in their purses during the long Sunday services at church to keep the youngsters calm. A usual Sunday service with a visiting preacher could be an all-day event, with an outdoor picnic lunch included. The womenfolk would pack enough lunch for themselves and those who might have "fallen on hard times," as my grandmother would say. Everyone would share in these dinners, called "Homecomings."

My mother would tell me stories of the moonshiners that would pack their cars and haul moonshine down Georgia Highway 9. The windy mountain highway became known as Thunder Road, because it was filled with the screaming sounds of car engines as bootleggers hauled their liquid gold to Atlanta and surrounding towns. The back of the cars were jacked up so that while loaded with moonshine the cars looked like a regular car. Patrol cars found it hard to distinguish between a regular car and a bootlegger's car. The only way to tell the difference was seeing the car when it returned from a haul. The back of the car would be jacked up higher than the front.

The old Dahlonega Baptist Church, located across from the Smith House, had a baptismal pool lined with copper made from old moonshine stills. Former moonshiners donated the materials after they converted from their sinful acts.

> **The Remedy: The Shine**
> *(The Doctor is in!)*
> 1 pint moonshine or whisky
> 2 boxes of rock candy
> 1 pint honey
> 2-4 lemons squeezed (depending upon flavor)
>
> Place the candy inside a glass container, such as a mason jar, with moonshine. Let the moonshine and candy sit overnight until candy is dissolved. Add honey and lemon the next day. Mix and let sit. When a throat tickle or irritation occurs, take a teaspoon or two and rest.
>
> *Warning- Do not operate heavy machinery while taking "The Remedy!"*

Smith House Pecan Pie

My grandmother, Thelma Welch, when she was older and no longer worked in the restaurant operations decided to start a side business of her own and bake her Pecan Pies. She sold her pies to my father on a

Smith House Pecan Pie
by Thelma Welch

- 1 (9-inch) unbaked or frozen pie crust
- 1-2 cups pecan halves
- 2 tablespoons butter, melted
- 3 eggs
- 1 cup sugar
- ½ teaspoon salt
- ½ cup dark corn syrup
- 1 teaspoon vanilla
- ¼ cup brandy
- ½ cup whipped cream

Preheat oven to 375°. In a small mixing bowl, beat eggs, sugar, salt, butter, syrup and cream. Stir in vanilla, brandy and pecans. Pour into pastry-lined pie pan. Bake 40-50 minutes or until filling is set and pastry is golden brown. Cool and serve.

weekly basis. One day my brother-in-law, Stan Bafile, stopped by her house to help her with a problem with in her house. As he was leaving, she stopped him and gave him a pie. He smiled thinking this was a big thank you but she said, "I charge Freddy $15 but I will sell it to you for $10."

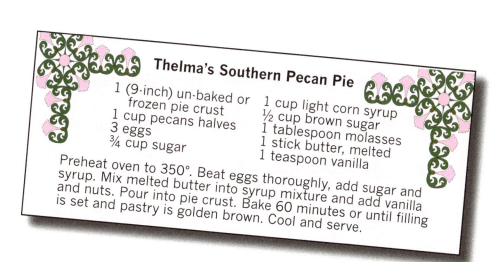

Thelma's Southern Pecan Pie

- 1 (9-inch) un-baked or frozen pie crust
- 1 cup pecans halves
- 3 eggs
- ¾ cup sugar
- 1 cup light corn syrup
- ½ cup brown sugar
- 1 tablespoon molasses
- 1 stick butter, melted
- 1 teaspoon vanilla

Preheat oven to 350°. Beat eggs thoroughly, add sugar and syrup. Mix melted butter into syrup mixture and add vanilla and nuts. Pour into pie crust. Bake 60 minutes or until filling is set and pastry is golden brown. Cool and serve.

Wagon Trains

Before the 1957 renovation of the Georgia State Capitol in Atlanta, two men had a bright idea for the dome of the structure. Thomas Bradbury, the man in charge of construction, and Gordon Price, a descendant of the founder of North Georgia College and an attorney in Atlanta, wanted to replace the traditional dome with an attractive and durable surface. Price had the idea of gilding the Atlanta dome like the Price Memorial building on the Dahlonega college campus. He could visualize the same appearance on a sunny day in Atlanta, with the gold shining in the light. This would commemorate the hard work of the miners in the North Georgia Mountains.

The two men took their idea to the local Dahlonega Chamber of Commerce and asked for a way to collect the gold. Bill Fry, who was the president of the chamber at that time, put the word out to miners' descendants for donations toward the project in a remembrance to their ancestors and the history they left behind. The Jaycees established a "Panning Day" (May 25) in an effort to obtain the forty-three ounces needed for the dome's completion. Through the efforts of citizens and donations, the goal was reached within two months.

Madeleine Anthony, a local historian, thought it would be fitting for an elaborate wagon train to carry the gold to the state capitol. On August 6, 1958, the wagon journey began with the forty-three ounces of gold carried in an old wooden box belonging to William Few, one of the Georgians who signed the US Constitution. Along for the ride were forty-three participants (men, women, and children ranging from 4 to 60 years old), fifteen mules, seven horses, seven covered wagons, two state patrol cars, and two dogs. Most of the men and women were dressed in attire which replicated the mining days; the ladies stood out by wearing old-fashioned bonnets and long dresses.

There were three camp sites along the 77-hour journey. The 3-mile-per-hour speed caused the state patrol cars to run out of battery during the journey, so two local members of the wagon train rode ahead on horses to warn on-comers of the procession. People lined the sides of the highway to cheer the train on. The last leg of the journey was on Peachtree Street, and all business came to a halt to watch this historic sight. Madeleine Anthony and Louella Moore presented the wooden box containing the forty-three ounces of gold to Governor Marvin Griffin. The governor hosted a barbecue celebration for the wagon train participants, and the scroll of the participants who gave their time and money is displayed at the Capitol to this day.

However, by 1977, nineteen years after the first application of gold, flaking occurred because of improper application. The Dahlonega Jaycees stepped up to the challenge again and started a fund

called "Make Georgia a Shining Example" to raise gold for the dome. Once again, a caravan of covered wagon trains assembled to visit each of the state's former capitols to collect gold. Thirty wagons started in Jekyll Island on May 1979 and traveled north. After six weeks, they pulled into Dahlonega. By November enough gold had been collected, and by 1981, the total remodeling of the dome was complete. Flaking on the capitol still occurs, but repairs are made immediately.

Smith House Banana Pudding

2-5-ounce packages instant vanilla pudding mix
4 cups cold milk
1 teaspoon vanilla extract
2-16-ounce packages vanilla wafers
9 bananas, sliced
1-12-ounce container of frozen whipped topping, thawed

In a large bowl. Whisk pudding mix and milk for 2 minutes, and then stir in vanilla. In a casserole dish or glass bowl, start making the layers; first lay down the wafers, top with bananas, and then the pudding mixture. Do three repeating layers, and then top off with the thawed whipped topping. Chill until ready to serve.

Ole Fashioned Banana Pudding

2 cups of milk
4 tablespoons flour
½ cup sugar
¼ cup sugar
4 eggs, separated
Pinch of salt
1 teaspoon vanilla
1 box vanilla wafers
5 bananas, sliced

Preheat oven to 350°. In two bowls, separate the egg whites and yolks. Set aside the egg whites for later use. In a sauce pan, add milk, flour, ½ cup sugar, egg yolks, and salt; bring to a boil. Whisk constantly, making the mixture smooth. Add vanilla and then take off the heat. In a small casserole dish, layer the bottom with crackers, then bananas, and lastly, the hot pudding. Continue layers until the pan is ¾ full. In the bowl with the egg whites, beat with a hand mixer until peaks appear. Slowly add ¼ cup of sugar until blended. Add the mixture to the top of the banana pudding. Cook in oven for 15 minutes, or until peaks are browned.

The Parade is Coming

I thought I was finished writing the final story for this book, when my mom told me another one that I knew I must include. She recalled a time that we had a float in a parade in Dahlonega. Elbert Gaddis worked for my grandparents, Fred and Thelma, and he wanted the Smith House to be represented in the local festivities. He came up with the idea of decorating a float with a wood stove and having participants dress in old-fashioned clothes. My grandparents agreed to the idea. The funniest part of the story is that instead of throwing out candy from the float, they used fried chicken legs! We all laughed, visualizing people being knocked in the head with pieces of chicken. I cannot believe that my grandparents went along with that idea.

Smith House Gold Rush parade float

Vanishing Georgia, Georgia Archives, University System of Georgia

Smith House Fried Bananas

4 firm bananas
6 tablespoons all-purpose flour
2 tablespoons sugar
1 egg, beaten
¼ cup milk
Confectioner's sugar
Frying oil

Mix flour, sugar, egg, and milk until smooth. Peel bananas and either cut into ¼ pieces or in half and then in cut down middle. Dip banana pieces into mixture and fry in a deep fryer until golden brown. Drain cooked bananas on a cloth and sprinkle with confectionary sugar. Can drizzle honey over the bananas instead of sugar.

Baked Bananas

Peel as many firm bananas as needed. Split the banana the long way and cut in half and place in a greased baking dish. Sprinkle with lemon juice and baste with melted butter. Sprinkle cinnamon, nutmeg, and brown sugar. Bake at 400° for 10-15 minutes or until brown. Top with vanilla ice cream.

Shirley Welch, Owner of the Smith House from 1970-Present

Smith House Blueberry Cobbler

My mother, Shirley Welch, grows her own blueberries for the cobblers every year. She has multiple plants that bring her in a plentiful supply of fruit that she uses for numerous recipes such as cobblers, jellies, and muffins. She does not use chemicals on the vines so her ingredients are 100% organic.

Smith House Blueberry Cobbler

3 cups washed fresh blueberries
½ of a lemon juiced

Preheat oven to 350°. Grease a glass baking dish with butter. Place berries into dish and pour lemon and ¼ cup of sugar and stir.

Topping
½ cup sugar
1 cup all-purpose flour
1 teaspoon vanilla extract
6 tablespoons cubed butter
Optional: 1 pinch of cinnamon

Topping: In a separate bowl, mix flour, sugar, butter, and vanilla with your fingers rub butter into the mixture making a course consistency. Top berries with topping and sprinkle with cinnamon. Bake for 25-30 minutes or until golden brown.

Smith House Peach Cobbler

3 cups sliced, fresh, or canned peaches
1 tablespoon lemon juice

Preheat oven to 350°. Arrange peaches on the bottom of a 10 x 6 x 1 ½ -inch baking dish. Sprinkle with lemon juice.

Topping
1 cup all-purpose flour, sifted
1 cup sugar
½ teaspoon salt
1 egg, beaten
6 tablespoon butter or margarine, melted

Topping: Sift together flour, sugar, and salt. Add egg to dry ingredients, tossing with a fork until crumbly. Sprinkle over peaches. Drizzle with butter. Bake for 25-30 minutes.

Smith House Apple Cobbler

7-9 medium apples, preferred Granny Smith, Fuji, or Golden Delicious
2 tablespoons butter
2 tablespoons lemon juice
½ cup sugar
½ teaspoon cinnamon
1 teaspoon vanilla

Preheat oven to 350°. Wash, peel and core apples and cut into ½ inch pieces and mix with lemon juice. In a sauce pan on medium heat, melt butter then add apples, sugar, cinnamon and vanilla and cook for 10 minutes or until tender. Cut off heat and let cool.

Topping: In a bowl mix flour, sugar, and spice. Cut cold butter with a knife into small cubes. Add to butter to flour and with fingers mix until mixture looks like coarse crumbs.

Butter a 13X9 baking dish and pour apples into dish. Sprinkle topping over apples and lightly drizzle melted butter on top. Bake in oven for 25-30 minutes or until brown.

Topping
2 cups all purpose flour
¼ cup sugar
1 stick or 4 ounces of cold butter
1 teaspoon apple pie spice (optional)
¼ stick melted butter

Smith House Strawberry Cobbler

1 quart of fresh strawberries
½ stick unsalted butter, cubed

Topping
1 cup self-rising flour
1 cup of sugar
½ stick unsalted butter, melted
½ stick unsalted butter, cubed

Heat oven to 350°. Wash and cut stems off the strawberries and cut in half. Sprinkle ¼ cup of sugar on strawberries and set aside. Butter a baking dish with the melted half-stick of butter.

Topping: In a separate bowl, mix flour, sugar, and cubes of butter. Work flour and sugar into the cubed butter pieces. Place strawberries in the buttered dish and top with flour mixture. Drizzle the left-over melted butter on top. Bake for 25-30 minutes, until crust is brown.

Gold Rush Days in Dahlonega
A Mountain Festival

Gold Rush is an annual event that occurs every October in Dahlonega. The beginning purpose was to stimulate tourism by recreating the event of the discovery of gold in 1828. Local people took pride in their attire, replicating the original clothing worn by the pioneers. Men wore overalls and grew their beards for months before the festival. Women sewed clothing for themselves and their children to wear for the weekend, and also greeted visitors with Southern charm. The town took on a new look, with wooden stages and businesses replicating the store fronts of the earlier days.

The first Gold Rush took place on October 8, 1954 when organizers such as Madeline Anthony, Doris Kenimer, Billy Moore, Newton Oakes, Hoyt David, Nina Head, D.C. Maxwell, Forrest Sisk and two previous owners of the Smith House, Bill Fry and Vernon Smith all came together as a council and planned an old fashion day in Dahlonega. As the group was discussing plans, Madeline's husband stopped by and said, "Why don't you have a Gold Rush Day to commemorate the gold rush era in Dahlonega." This idea sparked a 60 year annual tradition and is still going on. The planning committee came up with a fun day including a parade, booths made out of wooden slates, costumes, and games for all ages. Madeline was the first chairman for the event.

The committee headed up national campaigns to announce the festival. Newspapers and TV stations were contacted to broadcast the first "Gold Rush Day". Locals were requested to bring their horse drawn buggies and dress in their old fashion costumes. Panning for gold was the center of attention. Locals would use their buggies not only in the parade but carrying visitors to the Gold Mine and Museum located at the foot of Crown Mountain. The museum had been an old gold miner's machine shop and Bill Fry operated the museum. His passion was gold mining and gladly showed his guests at the Smith House the art of panning for gold. The museum and mine are no longer in existence.

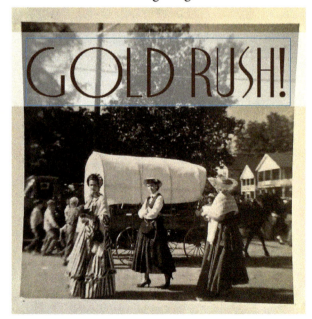

Script plays were enacted by local citizens replicating the finding of gold. One particular was a local, Billy Moore, started the day by riding in on a horse dressed as Benjamin Parks, the original finder of gold in 1828. He proclaimed riding thru the public square that he had found gold. The excitement started the day's activities such as the announcing of the Gold Rush King and Queen, longest beard, tobacco spitting, greased pig and pole climbing contest. Throughout the years other contests were added. A parade was a favorite local activity that took place on Saturday afternoon of Gold Rush. Sight-seers lined up for the beautifully decorated floats and waited for the treats to fly from the float's participants. Local children preferred to dress like the Indians, while the mothers were dressed as pioneers. Bonnets and long dresses with aprons attached were worn. Everyone scoured their storage to find a relic from the past to show at the festival.

Gold Rush
Kings and Queens

Each year, the title of Gold Rush King and Queen is awarded to a specific individual or couple. The qualifications for the title is to be a longstanding citizen of Lumpkin County and either a descendants of miners or a person instrumental in building the town into a historical landmark. The Dahlonega Jaycees chose from this strict guideline. The nominating of the King and Queen happened weeks before the festival. Fred and Thelma Welch, owners of the Smith House, were selected in 1993 for their commitment in growing a business on the public square of Dahlonega. They worked as a team which impacted the tourist growth. The Welches provided the yearly meal at the Smith House for the participants of past and present. Mr.

2014 luncheon for past and present Gold Rush Kings and Queens

and Mrs. Fry, previous owners, also were nominated. Mr. Fry was King in 1969 for his ongoing commitment to gold mining and the tourist industry. Mrs. Fry was Queen in 1974 for her commitment to civil organizations in Dahlonega.

Today, Gold Rush is always held on the third weekend of October. Visitors from all over the world travel to experience the days of past mining and a glimpse into our history. The Dahlonega Jaycees heads up organizing the yearly event. Merchants and citizens can expect more than 200,000 visitors to be on the public square that weekend.

Gold Rush is declared as one of the south's most favorite festivals in Georgia.

2015 luncheon for past and present Gold Rush Kings and Queens pictured with Jaycees and guests.

Photo by Kyle Wade

Annual list of the reigning Gold Rush King and Queens

Year	King	Queen	Year	King	Queen
1954	Ross McDonald	Nina Head	1986	Harold West	Jewell West
1955	Dave Summerour	Julia S. Dale	1987	Robert Ragan	Fannie Bell Ragan
1956	Robert Meaders	Maggie Meaders	1988	Bill Bellamy	Vi Pigg
1957	Gordon Parks	Sallie Parks	1989	John Owen	Margaret Owen
1958	John Ralston	Nancy Wimpy	1990	Fred Fitts	Faye Fitts
1959	J. Arthur Anderson	Mary Ann Christian	1991	Thomas Sanders	Margaret Sanders
1960	Buck Cochran	Mamie Chochran	1992	Robert Jenkins	Allene Jenkins
1961	Emory Brackett	Sevilla Bracket	1993	Fred Welch	Thelma Welch
1962	Reece Chapman	Jeanie Chapman	1994	Frank Early	Lucille Early
1963-4	Festival canceled		1995	John Crisson	Dorothy Crisson
1965	Joe Phillips	Amy Trammell	1996	Robert Green	Ann Green
1966	John Wesley	Lizzie Thompson	1997	Ralph Fitts	Kathleen Fitts
1967-8	Festival cancelled		1998	Woodrow Parks	Vee Doyle
1969	Bill Fry	Ida Phillips	1999	Bryan Whitefield	Bertha Anderson
1970	George Dover	Madeline Anthony	2000	Charlie Jackson	Maryetta Jackson
1971	Reese Crisson	Callie Crisson	2001	Fred Hood	Irene Hood
1972	Charlie Walker	AnnieMae Woodward	2002	J.B. Jones	Leslie Jones
1973	Will D. Young	Helen J. Potter	2003	Cam Cantrell	Pat Cantrell
1974	Col. W.A. Hedden	Effie Kate Fry	2004	Dan Davis	Dola Davis
1975	Lula Burns	Frank Abernathy	2005	CL Lingerfelt	Ann Lingerfelt
1976	Newton Oaks	Ella Ray Oakes	2006	Bill White	Ruth White
1977	Ernest Jarrard	Beulah Head	2007	Carlton Smith	Sandra Smith
1978	Desmond Booth	Nelle Young	2008	Ralph Calhoun	Elizabeth Cornelius
1979	Price Bowen	Myrtle Bowen	2009	Bryson Wilkins	Loretta Grizzle
1980	Charlie Jackson	Ottie Lee Jackson	2010	Larry Sorohan	Sallie Sorohan
1981	Guy Wimpy	Billie Wimpy	2011	Bill Lawson	Ann Lawson
1982	Raleigh Lee	Mary S. Jarrard	2012	Jack Anthony	June Anthony
1983	Elbert Gaddis	Bessie Gaddis	2013	Amos Amerson	Anne Amerson
1984	Bill Maxwell	Irene Maxwell	2014	Gary McCullough	Charlotte McCullough
1985	Travis Cantrell	Constance Thomas	2015	Clarence Grindle	Patricia Grindle

1993 Gold Rush
King Fred and Queen Thlema Welch.

Effie & Bill Fry in 1969,
when Bill was King of Gold Rush.
Effie Fry was Queen of Gold Rush in 1974.

1969 Gold Rush King Bill Fry on the left,
is pictured with Governor & Mrs. Lester Maddox.
Queen Ida Avery Phillips is on the right.

Stamp Mills and the Frank Hall Stamp Mill

Present day Frank Hall Stamp mill located at
Consolidated Gold Mine

The Frank Hall Stamp Mill

Frank Hall was well respected in the mining community. He was chairman of the committee of Mines and Mining. Dahlonegans referred to him as Captain Hall. He Patented the Frank W. Hall Stamp Mill.

Stamp mills are not a new invention only a perfected one used for specific purposes. There is evidence that the Greeks used the Stamp Mill around 3rd B.C. driven by water pestles and used well into the 1st century A.D. used for pound and hulling grain. The earliest Stamp Mill used for metals was by the Romans in the 1st and 2nd century. These stamp mills were hydraulic driven from the area supply of water. The first stamp mill recorded in the U.S. was at the Capps Mine in Charlotte, North Carolina.

A miner would deliver ore to the mill and unload it onto an ore car, then onto a screen called a grizzle (named after grizzly bear claws). The claws were equally spaced metal plates the ore would pass thru. The smaller ore passed through and down into an ore chute while the larger passed into the crusher. After crushing, the crushed ore passed over metal plates under the stamp battery and water ran down as a crusher. Thus turning into fine sand then taken to a recovery table, a sheeted table coated with mercury. The gold stuck to the mercury. The sand was once more taken to the stamp mill, pulverized again and then to the recovery table again. The table revealed the contents of gold and mercury then strained through a chamois. Then the gold was smelted down into blocks of gold bullion. Lumpkin County produced more gold in the 65 years prior to 1894 than any other southern state. -*Engineering and mining Journal, Vol 58*

1900s mill of the Crown Mountain Mining Company
where the stamp mill was run by electricity generated at power
plants on the Chestatee River.

Vanishing Georgia, Georgia Archives, University System of Georgia

BELL & APPLEBY.

HALL'S PATENT STAMP MILL,
For Wet Crushing.

ADMITTED TO BE THE

BEST, CHEAPEST, MOST EASILY
CONSTRUCTED AND CAPABLE

Of doing **MORE WORK** with **LESS WEAR** of wearing parts, and with **LESS POWER** than any Mill ever before made.

Hall's Electric Recorders for Stamp Mills.

☞ Send for catalogue, testimonial letters, prices, etc.

I AM ALSO MANUFACTURER'S AGENT FOR

Root's Rivited Spiral Seam Pipe,

FOR HYDRAULIC MINING AND OTHER PURPOSES.

LITTLE GIANTS.
LEFFEL'S WATER WHEEL.

The "Old Reliable," with improvements, making it the Most Perfect Turbine now in use, comprising the largest and smallest wheels.

ROOKWALTER AND OTHER ENGINES.

☞ Send for pamphlets and price lists of the Leffel Wheel and the Rookwalter Engine. This is the Cheapest and Best Light Engine in use.

SHAFTING, PULLEYS, HANGERS, ETC.

Powder, Dynamite and all
MINING SUPPLIES.

☞ Send for Prices and Catalogue. Correspondence solicited. ☜

FRANK W. HALL,
DAHLONEGA, GA.

UNITED STATES PATENT OFFICE.

FRANK W. HALL, OF DAHLONEGA, GEORGIA.

STAMP-MILL.

SPECIFICATION forming part of Letters Patent No. 276,582, dated May 1, 1883.

Application filed September 6, 1882. (No model.)

To all whom it may concern:

Be it known that I, FRANK W. HALL, a citizen of the United States, residing at Dahlonega, Georgia, have invented new and useful Improvements in Stamp-Mills, of which the following is a specification.

My invention relates to stamp-mills, its object being to improve their construction and efficiency in several respects, as more fully hereinafter described and claimed.

My invention is illustrated in the drawings accompanying and illustrating this specification, in which Figure 1 is a vertical section of my improved mill, taken through the mortar between the uprights. Fig. 2 is a perspective view of the mortar with part of the front removed, showing the die-seats. Fig. 3 is a plan section of the mortar, taken through the liners. Fig. 4 is a detached view of the cam, showing the mode of securing the same to the shaft; and Fig. 5 is a detached cross-sectional view of the mortar-flange, showing the mode of connecting the copper plate therewith.

Corresponding letters of reference are used in the drawings and in the following specification to facilitate the description.

A designates the uprights, extending at each side of the mortar from the base sill upward to the top of the framing; B, the base block on which the mortar rests; C, a longitudinal sill on which the blocks B rest; S, the cross-sills, extending beneath each upright A, and connected with and supported from the top of the frame by diagonal guy-rods E. It will be understood that these parts may be further duplicated in a frame for a battery containing more than one mortar or set of stamps, and the frame enlarged to any extent, without departure from the principles of construction constituting my invention.

The mortar M consists of the usual cast-iron box with open front, arranged to rest upon the block or blocks B, and held in position by a tongue, t, cast upon its bottom, and a corresponding groove in the block B, as indicated. The mortar thus rests upon its supports B between the uprights A, and is securely held in position by wedges a, driven between the top of the mortar and cleats b, bolted to the inner sides of the uprights A. By this mode of mounting the mortar and the construction of the frame, the guy-rods E are kept taut and the shocks of the falling stamps are transmitted through and absorbed by the frame, the force of reaction at the mortar being neutralized by the transmitted impulse of the direct blow. The details of construction may be varied without departing from the essential principle, consisting in so constructing the frame that the mortar shall rest upon cross-sills connected by chord-bars or their equivalents with the uprights, to which the mortars are secured, thereby affording a means of transmitting the force of the direct impulse back to the starting-point, so as to neutralize the reaction. The result is that so long as the guy-rods are kept taut the impact of the stamps is wholly neutralized and no injury to the frame ensues, and I am thus able to dispense entirely with the ordinary expensive foundations with manifest and great advantage in cost of erection, besides being able thus to arrange and locate the stamp-mill wherever otherwise most convenient, without regard to the foundation, besides which in actual operation there is a reduction in the wear and tear of shoes and dies.

I also regard as a feature of practical importance the permanent arrangement of a stage, F, extending horizontally outward from the uprights A and sustained by guy-rods f above the copper plate G. The stage affords a standing-place by which convenient access is afforded to the cam-shaft H, and at the same time serves to protect the copper plate from falling objects.

The construction of the mortar with a view to the retention and removal of the liners and the dies is clearly indicated in Figs. 1, 2, and 3. The front of the mortar is entirely open, excepting a slight projection, m m, of the front wall inward from each end, behind which end liners, l' l', are inserted, having their rear ends beveled, as shown, to rest against and engage the similarly-beveled ends of the side liner, l, thus mutually supporting and retaining each other in position.

In the opening of the front wall the front liner, l^2, is inserted, and held in place by the screen s, which is arranged to slide in vertical grooves formed in the edges of the wall m, and to be held by keys k, driven in the grooves alongside the screen. This construction, as will be seen, permits the ready removal of the screen s and front liner, l^2, the mortar being thus entirely opened at the front down to its floor. This affords convenient access to the dies and facilitates their removal. To the same end the dies or anvil-blocks are set in semicircular sockets open in front, formed by re-enforced portions r of the mortar-bottom. When necessary to remove the blocks for any purpose, the screen and front liner are taken out, and the blocks can then be moved forward on the floor of the mortar or replaced with ease and dispatch.

It is found that the liners l wear most rapidly in the vicinity of the dies D, and, taking advantage of this fact, I construct the liners with corrugated backs, with the thickened portions opposite the dies, as shown in Fig. 3, by which construction the weight and cost of the liners are reduced without lessening their wearing efficiency—a consideration of importance in view of the usual remoteness of the localities where such mills are used from points where such parts can be made or repaired.

The mode of securing the cam to the shaft consists of the ordinary taper key, n, engaging in corresponding slots in the cam and shaft, with the blind-key n' set quartering therewith, as shown in Fig. 4. The key n is concave on the side next to the shaft, and therefore makes its own seat and adds the additional strength and security to the cam without loss of time or uncertainty in the fitting.

The mode of attaching the copper plate G to the mortar is shown in Fig. 5. A flange, c, extends forward from the bottom of the mortar, to the under side of which I attach the copper plate by taper-headed bolts d, with an intervening strip of wood as a gasket or packing. By this construction a permanent connection is secured between the mortar and the copper plate, which always remains tight and prevents leakage in case the mortar settles.

The devices for holding the stamps out of reach of the cams consist of arms N, provided with semicircular bases arranged to rest in a groove cut longitudinally in a bar, O, bolted to the uprights A in front of the stems. The arms are held in place by a rod, to which they are pivoted; but in use they have their bearing upon the bar O by means of their semicircular bases and the groove in which they rest. The bases of the arms N are arranged eccentrically to the pivot-rod and the bearing-groove, so that when the arms are thrown backward out of use they remain in an elevated position held by the eccentric bases. The construction is fully indicated in Fig. 1.

I claim as my invention and desire to secure by Letters Patent—

1. In a stamp-mill, the combination of the uprights A, the mortar M, the adjusting-wedges a, base-block B, cross-sills S, and guy-rods E, arranged as shown, whereby the shocks of the stamps are transmitted by tensile action of the guy-rods to the uprights, and thence back to the mortar, substantially as set forth.

2. In combination with the stamp-battery and its plate G, the stage F, substantially as and for the purpose set forth.

3. The mortar M, provided with the re-enforce r upon its floor, forming sockets open in front for the insertion and removal of the dies, substantially as set forth.

4. The mortar M, constructed with open sockets in the base-plate for the dies, and a front open to the base-plate, and provided with a removable screen and liners, substantially as set forth.

5. The liner l, as constructed with plane front and corrugated back, the thickened portions corresponding with the portions of the dies in the battery, substantially as set forth.

6. The mortar constructed with open front between the projecting front walls, $m\ m$, the end and side liners, $l\ l'\ l'$, the side liner, l, being held in position by interposing the end liners, l', between it and the projections m, substantially as set forth.

7. The mortar constructed with a projecting flange, c, at the base, in combination with the copper plate G, secured thereto by bolts d and interposed packing, substantially as set forth.

In testimony whereof I have hereunto set my hand in the presence of two subscribing witnesses.

FRANK W. HALL.

Witnesses:
ALONZO C. JOHNSON,
LUTHER B. RAMSAW.

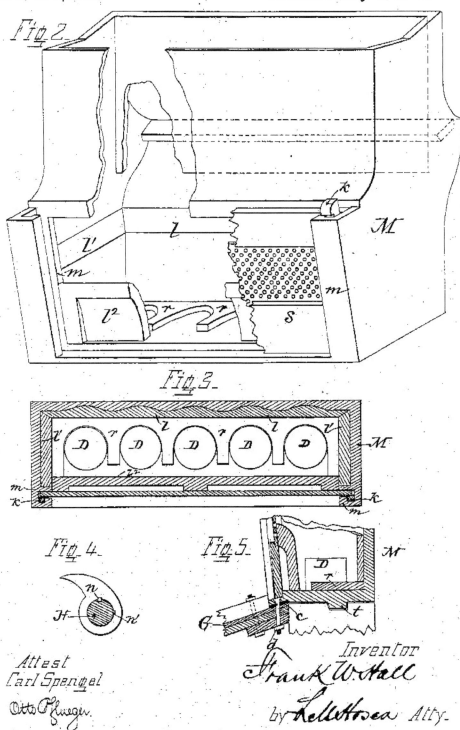

(No Model.)

F. W. HALL.
STAMP MILL.

No. 276,582. Patented May 1, 1883.

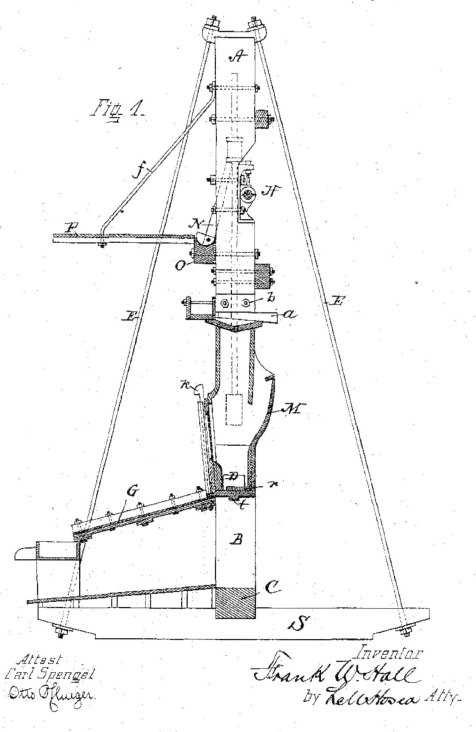

Fig. 1.

Attest
Carl Spengel
Otto Pflueger.

Inventor
Frank W. Hall
by Lell Hosea Atty.

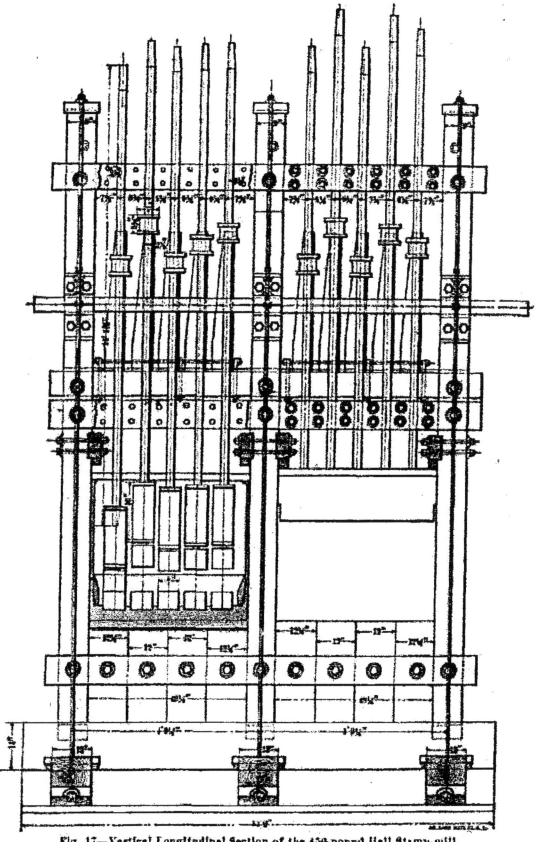

Fig. 17—Vertical Longitudinal Section of the 450-pound Hall Stamp-mill.

UNITED STATES PATENT OFFICE.

MAXCY R. HALL, OF FAIR MOUNT, ASSIGNOR OF ONE-HALF TO FRANK W. HALL, OF DAHLONEGA, GEORGIA.

STEAM-PUMP.

SPECIFICATION forming part of Letters Patent No. 259,136, dated June 6, 1882.

Application filed March 11, 1882. (No model.)

To all whom it may concern:

Be it known that I, MAXCY R. HALL, of Fair Mount, in the county of Gordon and State of Georgia, have invented a new and useful Improvement in Steam-Pumps, of which the following is a full, clear, and exact description, reference being had to the annexed drawings, forming a part of this specification.

This invention relates to an improvement in steam-pumps; and it consists in the structure and combination of elements hereinafter described.

In the accompanying drawings, Figure 1 is a longitudinal section of my improved steam-pump; and Figs. 2 and 3 are sectional views of modified forms of a double and a single acting pump, showing a different connection with the main piston-rod for operating the valve or valves of the pump.

The steam-pump is formed with the main water-cylinder A and the main steam cylinder B placed in alignment with each other and provided with pistons a and b, respectively, which are secured to the same rod, c. Alongside the water-cylinder A is placed a small cylinder, A', having supply orifices or pipes a' at or near its ends and a discharge-orifice, a^2, at a point midway between the supply-orifices. The cylinder A' is provided with two pistons, $d\ d'$, secured at a suitable interval apart upon the rod e, to form valves for the ports $c'\ c^2$, which connect the ends of the main water-cylinder A with the interior of the cylinder A'.

Alongside the main steam-cylinder B, in alignment with cylinder A', is placed a small cylinder, B', which is provided with a single piston, b', secured to the rod e. The cylinder B' is provided with a valve, m, which is connected by arms $m'\ m^2$ to pins $n'\ n^2$, adapted to slide in suitable openings formed in the heads of cylinder B when the piston b is moved in turn against the inner ends of said pins. The rod e is made to extend through the ends of cylinder B', and is provided at its end with a longitudinal slot, in which is confined the upper end of a stem, n, secured to the valve o of the main steam-cylinder.

The operation of the pump is as follows: When steam is admitted through the valve o at the left-hand port, the piston b will move to the right, carrying with it the piston a of the water-cylinder A. This movement of the piston a will cause the fluid or gas to enter through the left-hand supply-pipe a' and the port c' to the cylinder A, and the cylinder A will at the same time discharge through the port c^2 and the discharge-orifice a^2. This supply and discharge will continue until the piston b arrives at the right-hand end of its cylinder, when its contact with the pin n^2 will force the pin out and cause it to shift the valve m so as to open the right-hand port of cylinder B'. The piston b' will thus be forced to the left-hand end of its cylinder, and its rod e will shift the pistons $d\ d'$, so that the supply shall be admitted at the right-hand orifice a'. The same movement of the rod e will shift the valve o by means of the stem n and allow the steam to enter at the right-hand end of cylinder B to move the piston b to the opposite end thereof, where it operates the pin n' and the valve m in the manner already indicated.

With this construction the operations of the main pistons and the valve mechanism are made interdependent upon each other, so that one cannot work without the other. The piston-rod c, through the medium of the piston b and the pins $n'\ n^2$ and their connections, communicates the proper motion to the piston-valves $d\ d'$, and the rod e in turn, to which the piston-valves are secured by means of its connection with the valve o, communicates the proper motion to the piston b and the rod c.

In Figs. 2 and 3 are shown modifications of the pump. Fig. 2 represents a double-acting pump in which the supply-orifices a' are connected by a pipe, a^3, while the piston-valves $d\ d'$ are connected to the rod c of the main piston a by a lever, r, fulcrumed at or near the center thereof, and connected to the rod e by a jointed arm, r', at one end, and having its opposite end inserted in a longitudinal slot in the rod c. With this construction the piston-valves $d\ d'$ will be shifted only at the ends of the strokes of the main piston a, and the main piston cannot operate until the said valves have been shifted, the two being thus interdependent upon each other. Fig. 3 shows the same principle applied to a single-acting pump.

I wish it to be understood that I do not limit myself to the means herein described for connecting the rods of the main pistons and the piston-valves, since this may be done in various ways so as to secure the desired interdependence of one upon the other.

Having thus described my invention, what I claim, and desire to secure by Letters Patent, is—

1. The combination, with the water piston-valves $d\ d'$, of the steam-cylinder B', placed alongside the main steam-cylinder, and the valve m, adapted to be operated by the piston of the main steam-cylinder, substantially as shown and described.

2. The combination, with the main water and steam cylinders, of the rod e, connecting the piston-valve of the main water-cylinder with the piston b', and having a longitudinal slot therein, the valve of the main steam-cylinder having a stem fitting in said slot, and the valve of the cylinder B' having arms adapted to be operated by the piston of the main steam-cylinder, substantially as shown and described, and for the purpose set forth.

MAXCY R. HALL.

Witnesses:
W. K. HOPPER,
I. R. ARNOLD.

(No Model.)

M. R. HALL.
STEAM PUMP.

No. 259,136. Patented June 6, 1882.

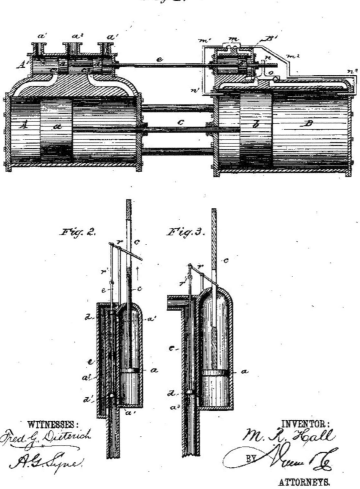

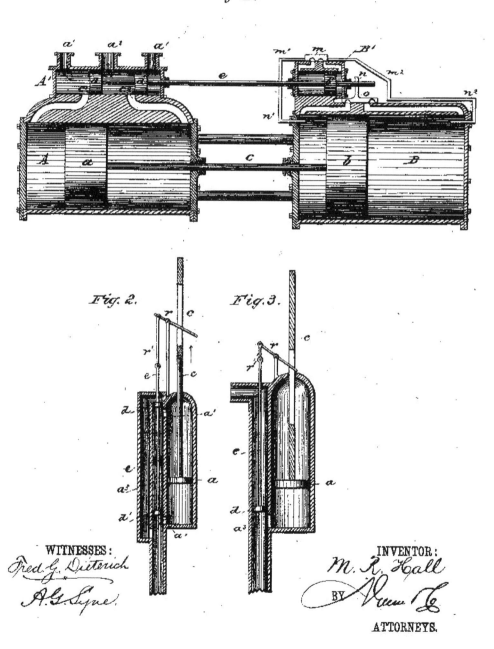

Picture Gallery of Old Dahlonega and its Gold Mining History

The following pages contain photos from the gold mining era that put Dahlonega on the map – of the *whole country*. All photos are from Vanishing Georgia, Georgia Archives, University System of Georgia. On the 1846 map below, Milledgeville is the capital of Georgia (1804-1868). Atlanta is not on this map by any of its names, including Terminus (1837) and Marthasville (1843).

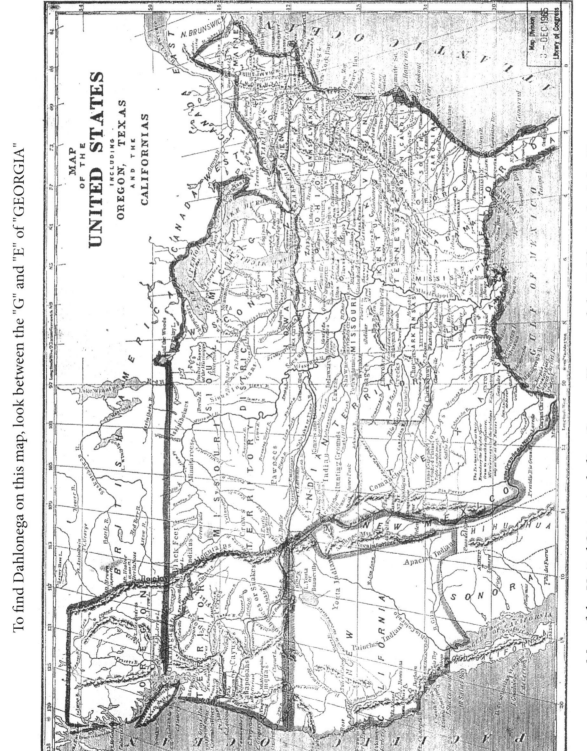

To find Dahlonega on this map, look between the "G" and "E" of "GEORGIA"

Map of the United States, including Oregon, Texas, and the Californias by John Haven, Haven & Emmerson, 1846. Geography and Map Division, Library of Congress, Washington, D.C.

Panorama of Dahlonega c.1899 (left side)

City of Dahlonega - 1899

Panorama of Dahlonega c.1899 (right side)

Dahlonega Branch of the U.S. Mint c.1878 before it burned
North Georgia Agricultural College cadets in formation

Wooden stamp on Gregory Mill erected on the Barlow Mines. Negative found in garret of the old Dr. Howard home built prior to the Civil War. Date of operation of this mill is doubtful.

Water wheel to run stamp mill at Baggs Branch Mine, Dixie Gold Mining Co., 3 miles south of Auraria, Lumpkin County, Georgia.

Gold mine stamp mill, Dahlonega, Georgia, 1890-1939

Stamp Mill (view from the other side)

Calhoun Mine, Lumpkin County, Georgia, 1890-1939

Dahlonega Mining Picture, Lumpkin County, Georgia, c.1905-1906

Mining dredge, Dahlonega, Georgia, 1890-1939

"Beal drill," east of Dahlonega, Lumpkin County, Georgia, 1900

Hydraulic mining, Dahlonega, Georgia, 1890-1949

Water-carrying trestle, Lumpkin County, Georgia, 1899
Several ditches were built to bring water from surrounding rivers to gold miners.
This high trestle was built to carry water across a ravine.

Crown Mountain Flume

Calhoun Stamp Mill, 1913

Thank You

I would like to extend my gratitude for all the people who helped me in so many ways to bring this book to completion.

This book has taken several routes. After running into many blocks, I asked my friend, Anne Amerson, for advise. The final version was constructed into short stories with recipes following.

I asked Gabriella Cubera to help me structure the stories and edit my information so the content would be enjoyable to the reader.

Chris Worick, President of the Lumpkin County Historical Society, for providing information on Free Jim and other pictures from his collection.

The Dahlonega Jaycees and Sallie Sorohan for providing information of the past and present Gold Rush Kings and Queens, and to Jimmy Anderson for information about the life of the Cherokee Indians here in Lumpkin County. He also allowed me to copy the original land lottery ticket of Lumpkin County to use in this book.

Robbie Niles who undertook the project of putting together the final book so that publication would be an easy process for me since this is my first book but not the last.

A special gratitude to my parents: My dad, Freddy Welch, who lived thru some of the history at the Smith House and provided me with real life history that took place while he was living here with his parents growing up. His knowledge provided me with accurate dates and added interesting facts to my collection.

My Mom, Shirley Welch, for starting me on this journey. She wrote the first Smith House cookbook, "Boarding House Reach," many years ago, and it was time for a new cookbook. Over her years here she has a vast collection of history facts that she allowed me to use in the book, and recipes from her own collection at the Smith House. Thank you for allowing me to publish the second Smith House cook book, and continue the legacy.

Last but certainly not least, my husband, Mike, and son, Evan Bafile. They are such an inspiration to me and giving me the time to complete the book. Mike spent many hours with me listening to the stories and giving his advice. He supports me in all the projects I undertake giving me wise council. Thank you Mike, for not letting me give up on the book and keeping me on this journey.

Thank you to my Lord and Savior Jesus Christ for being my rock on which I stand.

Notes